#MeToo, Weinstein and Feminism

"With #MeToo, Weinstein and Feminism, Karen Byle has created an indispensible resource for those working in gender studies, media studies, and cultural theory. In a moment when scholars and activists are wrestling with the cultural and political impact of #MeToo, Boyle carefully parses the differences between a "moment" and a movement, and importantly reminds us to think beyond the hashtag to consider history, political contradictions, and the limits of media visibility. With careful attention to gendered violence, witnessing and changing definitions of survivor/victimhood, the book is well-theorized, thorough, and nuanced, and it is essential reading for those trying to understand feminist politics within the contemporary cultural and media landscape, and how we got here."

—Prof Sarah Banet-Weiser, LSE, Author *Empowered: Popular Feminism & Popular Misogyny* (Duke, 2018)

"In a wonderfully readable, inspiring and authoritative account, Karen Boyle interrogates the ways in which what #MeToo has meant for men, has become a recurrent feature of media discourse. She shows us how media have framed #MeToo as a story of men, their morality and culture rather than as about sexual violence and male power. And how we are encouraged to read feminism through 'narratives of suspicion' as part of the problem, rather than the solution.

Karen Boyle shows us how mainstream media coverage of the #MeToo moment re-focused our attention away from violence towards women, towards the interests of men: men's right to sexual freedoms, and their right to have jokes and 'banter'. Offering analysis of media coverage Harvey Weinstein; Matt Damon's reflections on masculinity; and the ways in which male celebrity abusers have been allowed to 'hide in plain' sight; she eloquently unravels how media conversations about #MeToo have also functioned as (not so) subtle backlashes against feminism and women's rights. Her profound analysis asks us to reflect on the fundamental question: why do our media narratives STILL not ask why men rape?

A leading scholar in the field, and an original thinker, Karen Boyle has produced a beautifully written analysis which contains a politics of urgency and optimism; she articulates the ways in which cultures can be transformed through an understanding of the ways in which they function. This sense of possibility and opportunity makes her careful scrutiny profoundly significant, if we do want to make sure we learn the lessons from #MeToo. So, if we really want to understand why #MeToo happened and what we can do to make sure it is not needed again, then we need to take on board the insights from this definitive book."

—Prof Heather Savigny, Professor of Gender, Media and Politics, *De Montfort University*

"This timely book shines an important feminist light on 'Me Too' – which Professor Karen Boyle convincingly argues goes beyond 'just a hashtag' and can be considered as a key feminist movement of our times.

Throughout the book Professor Karen Boyle writes in a style that is both authoritative and sensitive, theoretically grounded yet incredibly readable, absolutely up to date with contemporary cases yet with roots firmly in the research and activism of her sisters (both academic and activists).

This book is a must read for anyone interested in understanding more about the Me Too movement. It crosses many disciplinary boundaries and will be of interest to sociologists and criminologists but also those in media studies, women's studies, law, social psychology and anthropology. Due to its accessible writing, activists and practitioners (counsellors, Rape Crisis staff and volunteers, sexual violence advisors etc.) will also find the book of interest.

Professor Boyle writes that she hopes to demonstrate how those in media studies might reintegrate and learn from feminist activism and interdisciplinary scholarship on men's violence against women. She can be congratulated in achieving this – providing an exemplary text demonstrating the crucial role of feminist media scholars in advancing theoretical and practical knowledge on pressing social problems."

—Prof Nicole Westmarland, Director, *Durham University Centre for Research into Violence and Abuse*

Karen Boyle

#MeToo, Weinstein and Feminism

Karen Boyle
School of Humanities
University of Strathclyde
Glasgow, UK

ISBN 978-3-030-28242-4   ISBN 978-3-030-28243-1   (eBook)
https://doi.org/10.1007/978-3-030-28243-1

This Palgrave Pivot imprint is published by the registered company Springer Nature
Switzerland AG.
The registered company address is: Gewerbestrasse 11, 6330 Cham, Switzerland

ACKNOWLEDGEMENTS

This book took shape over many conversations, conferences and collaborations. It first saw the light of day at a Strathclyde MediaComm Jam; different sections were tested out in presentations at the Universities of Glasgow, Wolverhampton, Sheffield Hallam and Liverpool; and debates at Strathclyde University Feminist Research Network, CAMEo, MeCCSA and WOW Perth propelled it forward. Thanks to all the colleagues, students and friends who invited me to these events and engaged with the work-in-progress, in particular: Michael Higgins, Catherine Eschle, Fran Pheasant-Kelly, Pauline Anderson, Yiannis Tzioumakis, Gary Needham, Lisa Kelly, Inge Sorensen, Kaitlynn Mendes and Helen Wood. Discussions with Gender Equal Media Scotland colleagues, the Applied Gender Studies class of 2019, and my fantastic PhD students, particularly Maja Brandt Andreasen, Daniel Massie and Jenny Wartnaby, who are all working on related projects, and have enriched my thinking. Rachael Alexander has been an incredible Research Associate and located many of the examples used in this book. Collaborating with Chamil Rathnayake on #HimToo (Chap. 5) was a joy and took my thinking in new directions; I am grateful for his generosity in collecting and sharing data. Susan Berridge's thoughtful reading of the draft chapters has helped me to sharpen my analysis and writing, whilst providing much-needed encouragement to help me over the finishing line. Ian Garwood's proof reading of the final draft has hopefully saved me from embarrassment and his support, both practical and emotional, has been phenomenal. To have Sarah Banet-Weiser, Heather Savigny and Nicole Westmarland reading the book in the final stages has been an incredible honour and inspiration.

The period in which this book was written was a very difficult one and it breaks my heart that my dear friend Kat Lindner is not at the finishing line with me: Kat, how I miss putting the world to rights with you. Without the support of all my family, friends and colleagues, it is difficult to imagine I could have got to the end of this book. Thanks in particular to Maureen McDonald and Churnjeet Mahn for getting me through one of the most difficult days; Kirstie Blair for being everything a line manager should be and more; Marie O'Brien for understanding, making me laugh and bringing out the Grand Duchess when needed; Sarah Neely, Sarah Smith and Elaine Liston for spas and fizz; Gav, Carleen, Ryan and Erin Boyle, Val Murray, Tracey Coleman and Lynne McFarlane for cheerleading from near and far; and Suzy Angus and Laura Montgomery who continue to be an inspiration. I have been so lucky to have had the unwavering support of my Mum and Dad, Eliz and Sandy, throughout the process: you are incredible. Mum & Dad, Michael and Margaret Garwood, and Jenny and Tony Neale have ensured the kids had a great time when I was stuck at the computer. Thank you all.

None of this would have been possible without the loves of my life, Ian, Alec & Carys. Thank you for reminding me what is important.

CONTENTS

CHAPTER 1

#MeToo, Weinstein and Feminism

INTRODUCTION

This book takes as its starting point reports from a number of women that self-styled movie mogul Harvey Weinstein sexually assaulted them. Jodi Kantor and Megan Twohey broke the Weinstein story in the *New York Times* on 5 October 2017 and the findings of Ronan Farrow's simultaneous investigation for the *New Yorker* swiftly followed (Farrow 2017a). These stories prompted an outpouring of victim/survivor testimony, most prominently under the hashtag #MeToo, connecting the experiences of Hollywood women to those of women in vastly different geographic and socio-economic locations. However, it is one of the arguments of this book that for the contemporary moment to affect radical change it is important to understand its relationship to decades of feminist activism, theory and research. In this introduction, I clarify how I am using each of the three key words in my title—#MeToo, feminism and Weinstein—and explain my use of the term victim/survivor, before providing an overview of the way these are brought together in the organisation of the book.

THE #MeToo MOMENT

We are in a moment when feminism is popular, at least in an Anglo-American context (Banet-Weiser 2018). This new-found popularity pre-dates October 2017 and a number of critics have documented how

1

K. Boyle, *#MeToo, Weinstein and Feminism*,
https://doi.org/10.1007/978-3-030-28243-1_1

feminist concepts and arguments have permeated mainstream media discourse in the 2010s. Kate Manne, for instance, has noted the increasing prevalence of "misogyny" in news headlines (2018: 31), whilst Nickie D. Phillips (2017: 13–15) found a 1871% increase in the use of the term "rape culture" in newspaper and magazine articles between 2010 and 2014. Other touchstones in accounts of feminism's resurgent popularity are Beyoncé's performance against the giant, illuminated word FEMINIST at the MTV Music Video Awards, and actor Emma Watson's speech at the UN Women #HeForShe campaign launch, both in 2014 (Banet-Weiser 2018: 6–9; Rottenberg 2018: 10–11). Merriam-Webster declared feminism the word of the year in 2017, identifying the Women's March in January, the release of the television series *The Handmaid's Tale* (Hulu 2017) and the film *Wonder Woman* (dir. Patty Jenkins 2017), as well as #MeToo, as key moments driving online searches for "feminism".

It is not accidental that these indicators of feminism's popularity are all centrally about the *mediation* of feminism—how feminism is understood in and through popular media texts and platforms. Indeed, in *Empowered: Popular Feminism and Popular Misogyny*, Sarah Banet-Weiser argues that popular feminism "generally materializes as a kind of *media* that is widely visible and accessible" (2018: 9). Banet-Weiser's cogent analysis points to the feminist work which can be done in and through the popular media, whilst also acknowledging the ways in which popular feminism can be profoundly ambivalent for a wider feminist politics, at least in part because of the emphasis on visibility over action. Popular feminism in this iteration is fundamentally about being *seen*—as a feminist, supporting feminist issues—rather than, necessarily, about *doing* feminism. Moreover, the feminisms which become popular—and visible—are those which "do not challenge deep structures of inequities" (Banet-Weiser 2018: 11). These are feminisms of the individual rather than the collective, what Catherine Rottenberg (2018) describes as neoliberal feminism. Like Banet-Weiser, Rottenberg is concerned with how feminism becomes a mainstream story and the ways in which this distorts wider feminist histories of activism, research and debate.

The popular mediation of feminism has long been a concern for feminist activists as well as media scholars. Women's liberation movement publications from the early 1970s consistently referenced "the media" as a site of possibility—and concern—for feminists. British movement publications often reprinted stories from the national press as sources of information about issues concerning feminists, whilst simultaneously debating the benefits and limitations for the movement in engaging with these same mainstream media organisations. For instance, the first issue of the Women's Liberation Workshop journal *Shrew* devotes a number of pages to the relationship of the movement to the "bourgeois press" which, it notes in its cover story, "has expressed a great deal of interest in women's liberation" (*Shrew* 1970). On the one hand, it was widely recognised that this kind of engagement could open up the movement to a wider range of women, a precursor of Banet-Weiser's concern with feminism's popularity. On the other, media representation was not always positive and feminists in both the UK and US were understandably suspicious of journalists' motivations and often frustrated by their insistence on individualising the collective ethos of the movement by constructing "stars" (Mendes 2011; Dow 2014; Sheehan 2016). As such, there has long been a recognition that the discursive construction of feminism has only ever been partly within feminists' control.

Although this may seem like an obvious point, it is one worth returning to in relation to #MeToo. As is well-known, #MeToo began trending after a tweet from US actor Alyssa Milano on October 15:

> Me Too.
> Suggested by a friend: "If all the women who have been sexually harassed or assaulted wrote "Me Too" as a status, we might give people a sense of the magnitude of the problem".
> (@AlyssaMilano, 15 October, 2017)

Within just 24 hours, 12 million Facebook posts using the hashtag were written or shared and within 48 hours the hashtag had been shared nearly a million times on Twitter (Lawton 2017). Milano's initial aim for #MeToo was to "give people a sense of the magnitude of the problem". In other words, it was discursive activism, aiming to change what "sexual harassment and assault" means by expanding the understanding of who its victims/survivors are. As a collectively produced story about sexual harassment and assault (Serisier 2018: 101), it has—in many ways—achieved Milano's goal, although, as we will see, a counter-narrative or backlash has existed alongside #MeToo virtually from the outset.

It is important to emphasise that #MeToo is indivisible from the media platforms through which it has circulated. For better and for worse, #MeToo is *networked* feminism: a feminism made possible by the affordances of the social media platforms on which it circulates. Echoing

Banet-Weiser's arguments about popular feminism and visibility, the very repetitions of #MeToo are at times read as constituting a movement in and of themselves. For instance, Me Too Rising (https://metoorising. withgoogle.com) is a fascinating resource which maps searches for #MeToo across time and place, allowing us to see patterns in the global development of the #MeToo story over time. However, Me Too Rising is presented as "a visualization of the *movement* from Google Trends": equating online searching for #MeToo with activism, and confining the movement to the platform. In addition, Me Too Rising also allows you to look at where #MeToo is trending at any given time, and these trends typically link to mainstream news outlets.

This example demonstrates that Me Too is not only networked feminism: it is also a mainstream news story, involving many competing voices attempting to determine, assert and limit the meanings and significance of the outpouring of evidence of gendered violence and harassment associated with the hashtag. These stories may—as Banet-Weiser's analysis of popular feminism demonstrates—do feminist work, but focusing simply on the most visible stories as representative of contemporary feminism is profoundly distorting. Visibility and movement are not synonymous, as the Tufnell Park Women's Liberation Workshop recognised in 1970:

> We can be so written about and give so many interviews that we can be deceived into thinking that there is a movement when all we're doing is dealing with the press and TV. (Tufnell Park Women's Liberation Workshop 1970: 4)

This is one reason why reading critiques of #MeToo can be a frustrating experience. Important points about the way the #MeToo story has evolved (including, for instance, the centring of economically and racially privileged US women in mainstream media coverage) are used to argue for the limitations of #MeToo as a feminist movement. When this happens, we allow mainstream media to define what feminism is, and miss an opportunity to hold them accountable. In this sense, it is important to investigate #MeToo not only as a facet of digital feminist activism (Mendes et al. 2019), but also as an object of mainstream media commentary.

Although what was to become #MeToo originated with Milano and her (unnamed) friend, Me Too as a feminist rallying cry and a *movement* did not. The Me Too movement was founded by Tarana Burke in 2006.

For Burke, Me Too was an intersectional demand for support and recognition for young women of colour who had experienced sexual abuse, as well as a statement of solidarity (Burke n.d.). Burke's version of Me Too was *not* initially visible in Milano's tweet, but Milano *did* subsequently acknowledge Burke's work, largely as a result of Black feminists amplifying Burke's voice online.[1] Burke has subsequently become a prominent figure in media debates about #MeToo. However, this should not lead us to the conclusion that these debates have entirely taken on Burke's intersectional demand.

In this book, I therefore differentiate between #MeToo and Burke's Me Too, with Me Too standing in for a long, if unevenly intersectional, history of feminist activism around men's violence against women. Indeed, the use of this simple expression—me too—within support contexts is documented in the UK by feminist scholars researching sexual violence pre-#MeToo (Royal 2019: Chap. 6), underscoring the importance of solidarity to the wider feminist movement against men's violence against women. Although my focus on #MeToo as a moment not a movement reverses the title of Burke's Ted Talk on the issue (Burke 2018), our concerns are similar. In insisting Me Too is a movement, Burke is reinserting a Black feminist history into a mass-mediated narrative which has marginalised it. In interviews, Burke has—as Serisier (2018: 116) notes—also differentiated between #MeToo and "the work", with the hashtag potentially (though not necessarily) creating the space for the work, but not being synonymous with it: this is a distinction between discourse (#MeToo) and activism (Me Too). Discursive activism can, of course, be part of a broader activist project, but activism is never solely discursive. Whilst both the movement/work and the hashtag go by the label "Me Too", as this book is primarily interested in what these mediatized narratives can tell us about wider feminist politics, I want to retain the distinction between the movement (Me Too) and the hashtag and stories with which it is now associated (#MeToo).

Women's testimonies are, of course, central to #MeToo, but these are equally indivisible from the media outlets and platforms which allow them to become a story. Arguably, what makes the #MeToo moment distinctive is less the speaking out—which women have been doing for decades as I discuss in Chap. 2 and as Burke's story demonstrates—but rather than the extent to which some of these stories have been widely *heard*. For feminist media scholars, *which* of these stories have been deemed worthy of this wider attention is significant. Ros Gill and Shani Orgad write:

> ...despite the excitement about MeToo's wide appeal and cross-class, cross-ethnicity and cross-race character, its *politics* and *aesthetics* are exclusionary in various problematical ways, echoing similar critiques about previous feminist movements such as SlutWalk (see Black Women's Blueprint 2011; Mendes 2015). Writing in *Feministing* on her experience as an LGBTQ person and survivor of multiple forms of sexual violence perpetrated within her own community, Jess Fournier criticized MeToo's "footnoting" of queer experiences, that is, their relegation to the margins of a conversation about pervasive sexual violence that definitely concerns us. The rapper Cardi B spoke powerfully about MeToo's favouring of a particular femininity that is "respectable" (Skeggs 1997) and "believable", leaving out women like herself (woman of colour, previously stripper, hip hop artist) who "do not matter". The overwhelming exclusion of disabled women from the MeToo movement has been another important criticism (Flores 2018; Wafula Strike 2018). (Gill and Orgad 2018: 1319)

I quote Gill and Orgad at length as their examples bear further scrutiny for what they reveal about what #MeToo *is* and the questions this raises about responsibility. Black women protesting against the rhetoric of SlutWalk could (and did) address their criticisms very directly to organisers of marches and events. As such, they could (and did) address people who were putting themselves forward as doing feminist work, to demand that they think through the implications of organising under this banner (Black Women's Blueprint 2011).

But when we critique #MeToo, who or what are we critiquing?

The articles Gill and Orgad cite are all, in different ways, concerned with recognition within the #MeToo discourse. Notably, their critiques are *simultaneous* with the emergence and circulation of #MeToo and are, in some cases, published in mainstream outlets: Flores in *Teen Vogue* (2018), Wafula Strike in the *Guardian* (2018). Arguably, this speaks to the possibilities of #MeToo in creating spaces for this conversation even as, both in personal exchanges and mainstream commentary, these are also challenged and shut down as Fournier (2017), in particular, argues. Again, this is reminiscent of Banet-Weiser's work, alerting us to the contradictory presence and erasure of an intersectional feminist analysis in the #MeToo moment, which points to the limitations of framing intersectionality as a politics of identity and recognition rather than structural critique.

However, most significantly for my purposes here, Gill and Orgad's account illustrates a certain blurring of boundaries between a movement and its representation.

Although this might seem pedantic, these are important issues for feminist analysis and activism as they suggest different sites for action and make different demands in terms of accountability and relationship to wider communities. One of the problems here is the *me* of #MeToo: in Milano's original "campaign", individuals using the hashtag were asked to share *their own* experiences (*Me*) to connect this to the experiences of others through the affordances of the hashtag and the acknowledgement of shared experience (*Too*). For feminists wanting to build on these experiences to make them part of a *movement,* it is therefore crucial to acknowledge the limitations of the platform and what is, therefore, likely to be missing from the body of evidence gathered under the hashtag #MeToo, as, indeed, Gill and Orgad do. Thinking about the limitations of the platform, for instance, opens up questions around digital access and literacy (Mariscal et al. 2019), about audience and surveillance (Megarry 2018) and demands acknowledgement of the policing of women online through abuse which is both racialised and gendered (Amnesty International 2018). That differing notions of "respectability" impact on which victim/survivors are constructed as believable (as suggested by Cardi B in the Gill and Orgad quote) is not specific to the way sexual harassment and abuse are discussed online, but it is clearly part of the context in which individual women decide (not) to post #MeToo (Mendes et al. 2019). These notions also shape the way individual testimonies are then taken up and amplified both within and across platforms.

This critique is important and the demands it makes are on those of us who want to use the individual testimonies to build analysis and action. However, there is a risk in presenting this as a critique of #MeToo, particularly given the very personal testimonies collected under the hashtag. This points to one of the central difficulties in discussing #MeToo: namely, who or what this term now represents. This is compounded by the fact that #MeToo is still very much in use and so its meaning is under constant renegotiation. At one level, it makes perfect sense to talk of #MeToo as a movement: the hashtag has galvanised literally millions of people (particularly women) globally to speak out about sexual harassment and abuse. The amorphous nature of #MeToo need not, in itself, be a barrier to identifying it as a movement given the long-history of "structurelessness" in feminist activism (Freeman n.d.). Moreover, in many high-profile instances, this speech has had concrete repercussions for perpetrators and posting #MeToo and other hashtags of disclosure have, in themselves, been transformational for some women (Mendes et al. 2019; Serisier 2018).

Yet, beyond the parameters of Milano's initial tweet, it is difficult to identify the core characteristics of #MeToo, not least because it has (as a hashtag) been taken up so widely by people who may share little else in terms of political philosophy or principles. No doubt partly because it began as a US-led, celebrity-oriented expression, #MeToo has been difficult to disentangle from the mainstream media representation of #MeToo. As such, I have found it more useful to think of #MeToo as a *moment* (which begins on 15 October 2017 and continues at the time of writing) and as a *discourse*.

One of the goals of this book is to situate #MeToo in relation to a wider feminist movement and a longer history of feminist activism which, of course, includes Burke's Me Too and the challenges it poses. But it is also to investigate some of the different stories about #MeToo which have been told in the 18 months since Milano's tweet and consider how these stories do (not) engage with feminism in that broader sense. A central theme running through this book is how feminism—and feminists—are popularly (re)constructed in mainstream media accounts of #MeToo. Part of what is at stake here are questions of expertise, speech, believability and authority—issues which I explore more centrally in Chap. 2, but which I preview in the next section by reflecting on the feminism(s) with which this book seeks to engage.

Feminism(s)?

Simply put, feminism is a movement to end sexism, sexist exploitation, and oppression. (hooks 2000: 1)

Bell hooks' definition of feminism guides the discussion in this book. It serves as a reminder that feminist theory can never be theory for theory's sake, but is theory which seeks to have a practical application in changing the world. As such, it should never be static, but continue to evolve: feminist theory is part of the feminist *movement*. This is certainly true of the feminist theories with which this book is most centrally concerned, theories which help us to: build a movement; understand and so challenge men's violence against women whilst also supporting women; and rethink representational practices. As such, I am concerned with interdisciplinary bodies of scholarship focusing on feminism itself, on violence as a feminist issue, and from within feminist media studies. I draw primarily on work developed in Britain and the US from the early second wave onwards. However, I largely resist the wave metaphor which is often used to periodise feminism, being more concerned with how particular ideas have developed within and across the periods, and even in the work of individual scholars associated with different waves. This is an understanding of feminism *in* movement: a feminist theory which is itself continually being refined and contested, not least in response to internal and external critique.

One important development across time has been the increasingly mainstream recognition of the significance of an intersectional analysis, that is, an analysis which requires a consideration of the ways in which gendered oppressions are differently experienced in relation to other structural forms of oppression, including race, class, age, sexuality, disability, religion and gender identity. Although intersectional analysis has long been a characteristic of the work of Black feminists in both the US (Collins and Bilge 2016; Taylor 2017) and UK (Bryan et al. 2018), the term intersectionality comes from the work of African American legal scholar Kimberlé Crenshaw (1989, 1991). Significantly, given the focus of this book, Crenshaw used the term to explain women of colour's experiences of the legal system in the US in relation to domestic abuse. The extent to which women's experiences of violence are inflected by race, location and economic privilege in particular have been recurring themes in the wider #MeToo discourse. As noted above, Tarana Burke's Me Too movement originated in the experiences of multiply marginalised victim/survivors who were young, urban, women of colour. However, whilst some multiply marginalised women have had a relatively mainstream platform in the #MeToo moment, this has not necessarily had the effect of shifting either (white) feminist or media practices overall.

In this sense, it is perhaps more accurate to talk about the feminist theories and activisms in this book in the plural. Whilst they are all united—to greater and lesser extents—under the definition proposed by bell hooks, the understandings of sexism, sexist exploitation and oppression and what is required to change these realities vary. One of the aims of this book is to interrogate the stories *about* feminism which are told through, and in response to, #MeToo. In this, I am informed by the work of scholars focused on the discursive histories of feminism(s) which asks who tells these stories, what purposes they serve and what is included/excluded in the models of feminist (re)generation which tend to dominate both popular and academic accounts of feminisms' histories (Hemmings 2011; Rivers 2017). Interestingly, though perhaps unsurprisingly given the age(ing) of many women associated with second wave feminist activism, there has been a flourishing of scholarship on feminist activism from the 1970s and 1980s, including through revisiting the significance of key texts and organisations (e.g. Bryan et al. 2018; Taylor 2017; Bronstein 2011; Graham et al. 2003; Bevacqua 2000). Whilst I am only able to touch on this scholarship in the book, it is an important inspiration in allowing for a more nuanced account of the relationship of generations of feminism—and feminists—than the media-friendly and individualist story of feminist conflict, which I critique in Chap. 2.

A final context it is important to acknowledge here is the growing scholarship on feminist digital activisms. Whether the turn to the digital represents a decisive shift in feminist organising and politics, mainstreaming intersectionality and offering sufficiently distinctive modes to merit the designation of a new—fourth—wave of feminism is debatable (Munro 2013). Like Nicola Rivers (2017), I am sceptical about the often ahistorical nature of discussions of the fourth wave, and the idea that feminist digital activism is uniquely and always intersectional is something this book disputes at various points. Rather than identifying either the period I am studying, or my own approach, as located within one or more of feminism's waves—something which, is, in any case, troubled by the fact that my research on #MeToo considers both the UK and US, where the waves have peaked and troughed differently (Evans 2015)—this book explores developments in feminist theory alongside contested understandings of feminist movement.

Why Weinstein?

In a book centrally concerned with feminist understandings of sexual violence and critical of mainstream mediations of sexual violence, it may seem contradictory that the only named individual in my title is (Harvey) Weinstein. Feminists in a variety of contexts in and outside of the academy have long questioned how best to represent abusive men, or those accused of abuse, and highlighted the danger of narrativising stories of sexual violence and murder such that perpetrators become celebrities and victims are forgotten (Williamson 2018). These questions are more fully addressed in Chap. 5, but there are a few points I want to make here to set up concerns which I address throughout the book.

First, the ability to speak about—and name—abuse in the public sphere has long been stacked against victim/survivors. Economic power, and the legal and disciplinary power money can buy, is an important part of that, as Ronan Farrow's investigation (2017b) of Weinstein's attempts to prevent women speaking to journalists about their experiences chillingly reveals. This made—and makes—reporting on the women's testimonies a risky endeavour, both for the women themselves and for journalists. Their experiences, in themselves, make the case for the continued importance of naming, but also makes me acutely aware of the boundaries around what it is and is not possible to say and how it is (not) possible to say it, particularly when criminal proceedings are (at the time of writing) still ongoing.

Regardless of the outcome of the criminal cases, Weinstein has come to occupy a particular place in the public imaginary around #MeToo that bears scrutiny. In this sense, the Weinstein of the title is *both* a real human who has been charged with a number of sexual offences against women and who has been publicly accused of many more, *and* a shorthand for referring to men accused of sexual assault in the #MeToo era. Of the real Weinstein, a 2019 *Sky News* documentary suggests that as many as 150 women have now come forward to speak out against him in some way, though I am bound to point out—as such documentaries also do—that he has continually denied all reports of non-consensual sexual contact.[2]

The second, more generic, meaning is best encapsulated in one of the original hashtag responses to the Kantor and Twohey article which encouraged women to name #MyHarveyWeinstein to call out workplace harassment:

> When did you meet YOUR Harvey Weinstein? I'll go first: I was a 17-year old co-op student and he insisted on massaging my shoulders as I typed. (@ annetdonahue, 5 October 2017)

This speaks to tensions around in/visibility with which this book is centrally concerned. The #MyHarveyWeinstein hashtag is of course possible only because Kantor and Twohey *did* name Harvey Weinstein in their *New York Times* article. At the same time, that Donahue does not name her own Harvey Weinstein speaks volumes about the difficulties women encounter in naming their abusers: the kind of harassment Donahue tweets about here is so endemic that women may not always know the names of the men who abuse and harass them in public places.

A final point in naming not only Weinstein but also other prominent men throughout this book is about trying to achieve a balance between giving voice to women and keeping both the structural nature of men's violence against women *and* the responsibility of individual men in view. Burke's simple but powerful statement—Me Too—enables women to speak because it acknowledges that our experiences are shared by others. It situates the individual in the conversation whilst also allowing us to see the bigger picture, thus meaning no one woman should carry the weight of that "Me" alone (although, as we will see, #MeToo has also become an imperative of sorts, in ways which undermine its radical potential). The collective voices of women also expose the structural nature of men's violence.

Naming Weinstein arguably undercuts this by placing one man in the frame. It is an approach that Burke has been critical of, observing that in the first year after the hashtag went viral there was "an unwavering obsession with the perpetrators – a cyclical circus of accusations, culpability, and indiscretions" (Rowley 2018). Rose McGowan, one of the most prominent women to speak publicly about Weinstein, also has misgivings: in her book *Brave* (2018: 115), McGowan refuses to name Weinstein and so perpetuate the linking of her name to his, referring to him only as "the monster". In a different context, exploring how film academics and curators should deal with the Weinsteins of the world (and the films with which they are associated), Rebecca Harrison (2018) argues that it is time to de-centre them once and for all, to "fuck their canon" and instead centre women and the stories which have *not* been told.

At the same time, naming is a means of insisting that individual men *are* responsible for their actions, even within a wider context where these actions are duplicated by other men and condoned by many more. Deborah Cameron (2017) writes: "We cannot put that shame where it belongs – with the perpetrators, not their victims – if we cannot describe the details of what was done and what was said". Although Cameron is referring here to the *what* of men's violence—the details disguised by euphemistic terms such as "inappropriate behaviour" and "sexual misconduct"—her point also applies to the *who*. Keeping Weinstein in frame is partly a reminder that his name *should* now always be yoked to #MeToo (though #MeToo should not always be yoked to him): it is a question of accountability. This is a different context than those addressed by either

McGowan (in her autobiography) or Harrison (who is making a point about teaching film). However, as Burke cautions (Rowley 2018), whilst it is important that men like Weinstein are held accountable, the movement cannot be equated with accused perpetrators. In this book, my focus is men's violence against women, women's responses to that violence, and media representations of victim/survivors, perpetrators and violence. In this context, not naming individual men would have a very different meaning: as I will argue throughout this book, context is crucial in thinking about gender, violence and representation. Telling stories about men's violence against women cannot only be about telling women's stories or we risk making men's violence exclusively a women's issue, letting men off the hook.

Focusing on Weinstein allows me to critically examine what has become a recurrent theme in writing about celebrity abusers and celebrities alleged to have committed abuse, namely that "everybody knew" about the allegations prior to them becoming news. Chapter 4 offers evidence of some of the contexts in which Weinstein's abusive behaviour in general, and his behaviour towards women in particular, had been publicly acknowledged prior to October 2017. I argue that these stories had a certain cultural value so long as they were not recognised as abuse. However, the repackaging of abuse as, for instance, artistic temperament or standard business practice, has also served a function for Weinstein and those defending him since October 2017, allowing him to argue that the problem is one of interpretation and changing social and sexual mores, not abusive behaviour per se.

However, there are limitations in making Weinstein the (anti-)poster boy of the #MeToo moment. Although Weinstein certainly occupied a position of power prior to the Kantor and Twohey story, in many ways he was always already understood as an outsider in the industry which made him (and which he made). Thus, Weinstein can now be seen as an individual monster without this necessarily leading to questions about the structures that protected him. As such, the focus on Weinstein risks displacing a feminist analysis of the #MeToo moment in ways I discuss in Chaps. 4 and 5, comparing media representations of Weinstein with those of other men accused in the same period.

Naming Weinstein also poses challenges for a writer (and publisher) committed to believing survivors, which I want to briefly reflect upon. At the time of writing, Weinstein has been charged with multiple offences but has yet to face trial. So in representing specific men, including Weinstein, my language is at times cagey. I have been writing about men's violence against women for more than two decades and challenging the assumptions which underpin our representations of who is doing what to whom has been a central theme in my work. Yet, when writing about prominent men without criminal convictions against them, I have also fallen into the trap of writing about allegations and denials. Reading Catharine MacKinnon's reflections on #MeToo were therefore a real light bulb moment for me:

> Culturally, it is still said "women allege" or "claim" they were sexually assaulted. Those accused "deny" what was alleged. What if survivors "report" sexual violation and the accused "alleges" or "claims" it did not occur, or occur as reported? (MacKinnon 2018)

MacKinnon's challenge is one I try to take up in this book. One of the reasons for naming Weinstein in my title is to challenge myself (and readers) to think about how we describe what women report he has done within the bounds of the law without—even if unconsciously—stacking the discussion against women from the start. As Deb Waterhouse-Watson writes, "while accused persons must be held innocent until proven guilty, a complainant must equally be presumed 'innocent' of fabricating the charge" (2012: 56) This is also what is at stake in the demand to #BelieveSurvivors. This hashtag was widely used in autumn 2018 to indicate support for Christine Blasey Ford and the testimony she gave in the hearings leading to Brett Kavanaugh's confirmation to the Supreme Court of the United States. Although commonly criticised for assuming that women always tell the truth and false allegations never occur, like MacKinnon, I want to assert that #BelieveSurvivors is instead about asking how the assumptions underpinning the way we think, write and act in relation to reports of sexual assault privilege victim/survivors or perpetrators from the outset. Believing survivors—like describing women's *reports* (rather than allegations)—is about reorienting our discourse so that there is a presumption that women are, as Waterhouse-Watson (2012: 56) suggests, "innocent" of "fabricating that charge" to replace the long-dominant presumption that women lie. This presumption will not always be borne out in any individual case, but neither—of course—is the presumption that women lie/allege and men tell the truth/deny. This is just one of the tried and tested formulations for writing about men's violence against women (and children) which this book seeks to interrogate, and Weinstein helps me to do this.

VICTIMS AND SURVIVORS

There is considerable debate in feminist scholarship and activism about the use of the terms "victim" and "survivor" to describe those (especially women) who have experienced sexual and other forms of gender-based violence. These debates typically hinge on agency, with the term "survivor" often being preferred as it offers a more agentic identity and the possibility of recognising women's active resistance (Kelly 1988). However, feminists have also cautioned against seeing these terms as binaries and so reinforcing the stigma of victimisation (Jordan 2004: 12). As our knowledge of women's experiences of sexual and other forms of gender-based violence has expanded, we have also come to recognise that survival is not a destination but a process (Kelly et al. 1996). This makes sense, for instance, of oft-repeated claims that a criminal trial or media coverage may constitute a second victimisation: claims which are highly pertinent in the context of this book.

The extensive media coverage of #MeToo had concrete implications for many victim/survivors, not only those who were most visible in public discourse. For instance, the Rape Crisis network in England and Wales received a 28% increase in calls in the two weeks after the Weinstein story broke (Moss 2018); whilst, in the US, the Rape, Abuse and Incest National Network reported a 23% rise in calls to their crisis hotline in October–December 2017 compared to the same period in 2016 (Seales 2018). Whilst there may be a positive element to this—with the coverage enabling people to recognise their experiences and seek support—at the same time, wall-to-wall coverage of sexual assault can be retraumatising (Muller 2018), not least given the persistence of victim-blaming narratives (Royal 2019).

#MeToo allows us to see that victimisation and survival are moving points on continuum rather than binary and all-consuming identities (Kelly et al. 1996) An individual's movement across the continuum is not uni-directional or strictly chronological, such that, for instance, victim *becomes* survivor (Boyle 2019). In this book, I have therefore used the term victim/survivor throughout as a means of acknowledging that experiences of victimisation and survival are dynamic and contextual.

OUTLINE OF THE CHAPTERS

The remainder of the book is organised into four substantive chapters, each tracing a key theme in feminist theorising and organising. In the next chapter, I situate the "silence breakers" of the #MeToo moment in a longer feminist history of speaking out about men's violence. This allows me to explore the *function* of victim/survivor testimony for feminist theory and organising in relation both to histories of feminist consciousness-raising and engagements with mainstream media. In the final section of this chapter, I analyse how key moments in the development of the interrelated Weinstein and #MeToo stories were picked up, extended and represented in mainstream media. Setting up concerns I will return to throughout the book, I examine how feminism and feminists feature in this coverage. This allows me to highlight the simultaneity of #MeToo and the backlash against its feminist orientations and challenges.

Chapter 3 is centrally concerned with how feminist theory has advanced our understanding of the *structural* nature of men's violence against women and the pervasive nature of that violence in women's lives. Liz Kelly's formulation of the *continuum* of sexual violence is the touchstone for this chapter which explores different ways in which #MeToo has rendered the connections between women, between different types of sexual violence and harassment, and between different men, more and less legible.

Where Chaps. 2 and 3 are oriented around women's experiences and testimonies, and how these are rendered in/credible in mainstream discourse, Chaps. 4 and 5 are oriented around (alleged) perpetrators and bystanders. Chapter 4 examines the oft-repeated claim about Weinstein and others (including, in the UK context, Jimmy Savile) that "everybody knew" about the way they behaved. It situates this claim in relation to feminist analyses of rape culture, but adds to this a consideration of the cultural (and, to a lesser extent, affective) *value* of men's sexual violence against women in and for the screen industries in particular. Chapter 5 then moves on to consider what #MeToo has meant for men. This chapter begins with a consideration of male victims of sexual assault, before considering how narratives of male victimisation have also been appropriated by (alleged) perpetrators, focusing on the Brett Kavanaugh Supreme Court nomination hearings which took place almost exactly one year after the *New York Times* published Kantor and Twohey's article about Weinstein. This is juxtaposed with the way Weinstein has been represented, and in exploring this difference, I draw both on Kate Manne's

(2018) discussion of himpathy, and on broader feminist debates about the "othering" of male perpetrators of gender violence.

In the book as a whole, I aim to demonstrate the advantages of understanding #MeToo historically and contextually. My hope is that, by insisting that we cannot conflate the media with the movement, this book offers one model for how those of us in media disciplines in particular might reintegrate, and so learn from, decades of feminist activism and interdisciplinary scholarship on men's violence against women.

NOTES

1. Tarana Burke has addressed her role in the movement and the hashtag in many commentaries, including, but by no means limited to, her Twitter posts @TaranaBurke. A thread on 21 February 2018, which I discuss in the next chapter, addresses these issues.
2. *Harvey Weinstein: The Fall of the King of Hollywood*, Sky News, 2019. The full documentary is available here: https://www.youtube.com/watch?v=GESBI9pWWmI, Accessed 25 April 2019.

REFERENCES

Amnesty International. 2018. *Toxic Twitter – A Toxic Place for Women*, March. https://www.amnesty.org/en/latest/research/2018/03/online-violence-against-women-chapter-1/. Accessed 25 April 2019.

Banet-Weiser, Sarah. 2018. *Empowered: Popular Feminism and Popular Misogyny*. Durham: Duke.

Bevacqua, Maria. 2000. *Rape on the Public Agenda: Feminism and the Politics of Sexual Assault*. Boston: Northeastern University Press.

Black Women's Blueprint. 2011. An open letter from Black women to SlutWalk organizers. Reprinted in: *Huffington Post*, 27 September 2011. https://www.huffpost.com/entry/slutwalk-black-women_b_980215 Accessed 22 January 2019.

Boyle, Karen. 2019. What's in a name? Theorising the inter-relationships of gender and violence. *Feminist Theory* 20 (1): 19–68.

Bronstein, Carolyn. 2011. *Battling Pornography: The American Feminist Anti-Pornography Movement, 1976–1986*. New York: Cambridge University Press.

Bryan, Beverley, Stella Dadzie and Suzanne Scarfe. 2018. *The Heart of the Race: Black Women's Lives in Britain*. Second Edition. London & New York: Verso.

Burke, Tarana. 2018. Me Too is a movement, not a moment. Ted Talk, November. https://www.ted.com/talks/tarana_burke_me_too_is_a_movement_not_a_moment. Accessed 22 January 2019.

Burke, Tarana. n.d. The inception. *Me Too.* https://metoomvmt.org/the-inception/. Accessed 2 April 2019.

Cameron, Deborah. 2017. On being explicit. *Language: A Feminist Guide* (Blog). 19 December https://debuk.wordpress.com/2017/12/19/on-being-explicit/. Accessed 20 May 2019.

Collins, Patricia Hill and Sirma Bilge. 2016. *Intersectionality.* Cambridge: Polity.

Crenshaw, Kimberlé Williams. 1989. Demarginalizing the intersection of race and sex: a Black feminist critique of anti-discrimination doctrine, feminist theory, and anti-racist politics. *The University of Chicago Legal Forum* 140: 139–167.

Crenshaw, Kimberlé Williams. 1991. Mapping the margins: intersectionality, identity politics, and violence against women of color. *Stanford Law Review* 43: 1241–1299.

Dow, Bonnie J. 2014. *Watching Women's Liberation 1970: Feminism's Pivotal Year on the Network News.* Urbana, Chicago, Springfield: University of Illinois Press.

Evans, Elizabeth. 2015. *The Politics of Third Wave Feminisms.* Basingstoke: Palgrave Macmillan.

Farrow, Ronan. 2017a. From aggressive overtures to sexual assault: Harvey Weinstein's accusers tell their stories. *New Yorker,* 10 October.

Farrow, Ronan. 2017b. Harvey Weinstein's army of spies. *New Yorker,* 6 November.

Flores, Emily. 2018. The #MeToo movement hasn't been inclusive of the disability community. *Teen Vogue,* 24 April. https://www.teenvogue.com/story/the-metoo-movement-hasnt-been-inclusive-of-the-disability-community. Accessed 24 February 2019.

Fournier, Jess. 2017. #MeToo: don't make trans and queer survivors a footnote. *Feministing,* 31 October. http://feministing.com/2017/10/31/metoo-dont-make-trans-and-queer-survivors-a-footnote/. Accessed 26 February 2019.

Freeman, Jo. (n.d.) The tyranny of structurelessness. https://www.jofreeman.com/joreen/tyranny.htm. Accessed 26 February 2019.

Gill, Rosalind and Shani Orgad. 2018. The shifting terrain of sex and power: from the "sexualization of culture" to #MeToo. *Sexualities,* 21 (8): 1313–1324.

Graham, Helen, Ann Kaloski, Ali Neilson and Emma Robertson. eds. 2003. *The Feminist Seventies.* York: Raw Nerve Books.

Harrison, Rebecca. 2018. Fuck the canon (or, how do you solve a problem like Von Trier): Teaching, screening and writing about cinema in the age of #MeToo. *Mai: Feminism and Visual Culture,* November 9: https://maifeminism.com/fuck-the-canon-or-how-do-you-solve-a-problem-like-von-trier-teaching-screening-and-writing-about-cinema-in-the-age-of-metoo/, Accessed 25 April 2019.

Hemmings, Clare. 2011. *Why Stories Matter: The Political Grammar of Feminist Theory.* Durham and London: Duke.

hooks, bell. 2000. *Feminism is for Everybody: Passionate Politics.* London: Pluto.

Jordan, Jan. 2004. *The Word of a Woman? Police, Rape and Belief.* Hampshire: Palgrave Macmillan.

Kantor, Jodi and Megan Twohey. 2017. Harvey Weinstein paid off sexual harassment accusers for decades. *New York Times*, 5 October.

Kelly, Liz. 1988. *Surviving Sexual Violence.* Cambridge: Polity.

Kelly, Liz, Sheila Burton and Linda Regan. 1996. Beyond victim or survivor: sexual violence, identity and feminist theory and practice. In *Sexualizing the Social: Power and the Organization of Sexuality*, eds. Lisa Adkins and Vicki Merchant, 77–101. Basingstoke: Macmillan.

Lawton, Georgina. 2017. #MeToo is here to stay. *Guardian*, 28 October.

MacKinnon, Catharine. 2018. #MeToo has done what the law could not. *New York Times*, 4 February.

Manne, Kate. 2018. *Down Girl: The Logic of Misogyny.* New York & Oxford: Oxford University Press.

Mariscal, Judith, Gloria Mayne, Urvashi Aneja and Alina Sorgner. 2019. Bridging the gender digital gap. *Economics: The Open-Access, Open-Assessment E-Journal* 13 (9): 1–12.

McGowan, Rose. 2018. *Brave.* London: HQ.

Megarry, Jessica. 2018. Under the watchful eyes of men: Theorising the implications of male surveillance practices for feminist activism on social media. *Feminist Media Studies* 18 (6): 1070–1085.

Mendes, Kaitlynn. 2011. *Feminism in the News: Representations of the Women's Movement Since the 1960s.* London: Palgrave.

Mendes, Kaitlynn. 2015. *SlutWalk: Feminist Activism and the Media.* Cham: Palgrave Macmillan.

Mendes, Kaitlynn, Jessica Ringrose and Jessalynn Keller. 2019. *Digital Feminist Activism: Girls and Women Fight Back Against Rape Culture.* Oxford: Oxford University Press.

Merriam-Webster. 2017. Merriam-Webster's 2017 words of the year. https://www.merriam-webster.com/words-at-play/word-of-the-year-2017-feminism/feminism. Accessed 25 February 2019.

Moss, Rachel. 2018. If you found #MeToo triggering, this new mental health advice may help. *HuffPost (UK)*, 6 March. https://www.huffingtonpost.co.uk/entry/mental-health-charity-issues-advice-to-sexual-abuse-survivors-finding-media-coverage-difficult_uk_5a9d5a71e4b0479c02555b0f. Accessed 10 June 2019.

Muller, Justyna. 2018. Self-care techniques for women impacted by exposure to sexual violence media coverage. (Guidelines.) Mental Health Foundation/Rape Crisis England and Wales/Support After Rape and Sexual Violence Leeds. 5 March. https://www.mentalhealth.org.uk/publications/self-care-techniques-women-impacted-exposure-sexual-violence-media-coverage. Accessed 10 June 2019.

Munro, Ealasaid. 2013. Feminism: a fourth wave? *Political Insight* 4 (2): 22–25.

Phillips, Nickie D. 2017. *Beyond Blurred Lines: Rape Culture in Popular Media*. Lanham: Rowman and Littlefield.

Rivers, Nicola. 2017. *Postfeminism (s) and the Arrival of the Fourth Wave: Turning Tides*. Cham: Palgrave Macmillan.

Rottenberg, Catherine. 2018. *The Rise of Neoliberal Feminism*. London & New York: Oxford University Press.

Rowley, Liz. 2018. The architect of #MeToo says the movement has lost its way. *The Cut*, 23 October. https://www.thecut.com/2018/10/tarana-burke-me-too-founder-movement-has-lost-its-way.html. Accessed 10 June 2019.

Royal, Kathryn. 2019. *"It's Like Wallpaper": Victim-blaming, Sexual Violence and the Media*. Unpublished PhD thesis: University of Durham.

Seales, Rebecca. 2018. What has #MeToo actually changed? *BBC News*, 12 May. https://www.bbc.co.uk/news/world-44045291. Accessed 10 June 2019.

Serisier, Tanya. 2018. *Speaking Out: Feminism, Rape and Narrative Politics*. Cham: Palgrave Macmillan.

Sheehan, Rebecca J. 2016. "If we had more like her we would no longer be the unheard majority": Germaine Greer's reception in the United States. *Australian Feminist Studies* 31 (87): 62–77.

Shrew. 1970. Bourgeois press. *Shrew* 1: 1–3.

Skeggs, Beverley. 1997. *Formations of Class and Gender: Becoming Respectable*. Cham: Palgrave Macmillan.

Taylor, Keeanga-Yamahtta. ed. 2017. *How We Get Free: Black Feminism and the Combahee River Collective*. Chicago: Haymarket Books.

Tufnell Park Women's Liberation Workshop. 1970. Final word on the media. *Shrew* 1: 4–5.

Wafula Strike, Anne. 2018. Disabled women see #MeToo and think: what about us? *Guardian*, 8 March.

Waterhouse-Watson, Deb. 2012. Framing the victim: sexual assault and Australian footballers on television. *Australian Feminist Studies* 27 (71): 55–70.

Williamson, Terrion L. 2018. What does that make you? Public narration and the serial murders of Black women. In *Where Freedom Starts: Sex, Power, Violence, #MeToo*, A Verso Report: 42–48.

CHAPTER 2

Silence Breaking

INTRODUCTION

In December 2017, *Time* magazine named "The Silence Breakers"—the women (and some men) speaking out about sexual harassment in workplaces—their "person" of the year. In the editorial explaining this choice, *Time*'s editor-in-chief identifies the "individual acts of courage" which initiated what was to become "a hashtag, a movement, a reckoning" (Felsenthal 2017). In this way, Felsenthal identifies both the individual and collective importance of "the silence breakers", but the conclusion of his editorial also gestures towards some of the tensions which are inherent in the silence breaking metaphor, acknowledging that 2017 was not the year when these women necessarily broke their silence, but rather when "open secrets" and "moving whisper networks" moved onto social media and "push[ed] us all to stop accepting the unacceptable".

The *Time* story is a useful entry into the concerns of this chapter as it simultaneously highlights the power—and limitations—of speech, the importance of both social media and legacy media in giving voice, and prompts the question as to whether it is the *silence* which has been broken or a cultural inability to *listen* to victim/survivor speech. Actor Ashley Judd—one of the first women to publicly name Harvey Weinstein as an abuser—is quoted in the opening paragraphs of the *Time* story making exactly this point: "I started talking about Harvey the minute that it happened" (Zacharek et al. 2017). Judd had been talking about Weinstein since 1997 within her own networks, but it was her inclusion in Jodi

© The Author(s) 2019
K. Boyle, *#MeToo, Weinstein and Feminism*,
https://doi.org/10.1007/978-3-030-28243-1_2

Kantor and Megan Twohey's *New York Times* exposé, alongside other women who reported experiencing or witnessing Weinstein's abuse, that propelled her speech into the public realm.

Notably, part of the reason the Weinstein story had not previously been made public was the inclusion of non-disclosure agreements in Weinstein's settlements with those women who did raise complaints about his behaviour or seek legal redress. In this context, that investigative journalism was the genre in which the story could finally be publicly told is significant, and Kantor and Twohey's piece (2017) and subsequent reporting by Ronan Farrow (2017a, b) are at pains to establish the corroborating evidence their stories are built on. These reporters acknowledge the personal risks their sources are taking in speaking out, even as the reporters assert (and benefit from) the public importance of that speech. Farrow (2017a) also acknowledges the motivations of the women in speaking to him ("because they hoped to protect other women in the future"), as well as the cultural conditions which enabled them to speak out, including the slew of stories about public figures, including Donald Trump, Bill Cosby, Bill O'Reilly and Roger Ailes, which preceded the Weinstein case. Speech begets speech, but it is the *mediation* of that speech which is key to its success. Moreover, it is significant that the *Time* editorial positions silence breaking as generative of a *reckoning*, opening up questions about what this speech should mean for perpetrators which I pick up later in the book.

The "silence breakers" in the *Time* article are not all linked to the Weinstein exposé however, and I want to briefly discuss the initiators of Me Too and #MeToo to demonstrate some rather different forms and functions of speech which are collapsed in the term "silence breakers". In the story, Tarana Burke (n.d.) tells of the Me Too movement's origins, it is her *failure* to listen and to speak in response to a young Black girl's disclosure of sexual assault which inspires her activism. Burke painfully acknowledges that she "wanted no part" of the girl's disclosure. She writes "the emotions welling inside of me ran the gamut" and she "literally could not take it anymore". Although she redirected the girl, Heaven, to another counsellor, she acknowledges that her failure to listen haunts her: "The shock of being rejected, the pain of opening a wound only to have it abruptly closed again—it was all on her face". She continues:

> I watched her walk away from me as she tried to recapture her secrets and tuck them back into their hiding place. I watched her put her mask back on and go back into the world like she was all alone and I couldn't even bring myself to whisper….me too. (Burke, n.d.)

Burke's powerful writing forces us to recognise the emotional costs of both speaking out and listening, acknowledging the power and difficulty of solidarity. This interpersonal failure is, however, transformed into activism which has both therapeutic and advocacy functions "specific to the needs of different communities" (me too, n.d.). This is what Burke (2018) refers to as "the work" and I will argue that there are resonances, as well as dissonances, here with accounts of speaking out as the privileged site through which feminist analysis of sexual violence was developed through the 1970s. Crucially, for both Burke and those involved in the 1970s speak outs, speech is not a political end in itself but rather initiates the development of a public-facing, structural, political analysis.

Compare this with Alyssa Milano's tweet in the aftermath of the Weinstein revelations which, as detailed in Chap. 1, initiated #MeToo. It is the orientation and function of Milano's speaking out which interests me here. Like Burke, Milano positions herself *within* a community of victim/survivors through her statement "me too" and (again like Burke) does not—at least in her initial tweet—give details of her own experience. Rather, this is a jumping-off point for establishing commonalities with other "women who have been sexually harassed or assaulted". Milano's address is not solely to victim/survivors, as the explicit intent of these speech acts is to "give people a sense of the magnitude of the problem" (@AlyssaMilano, 15 October 2017). This is speaking out as awareness-raising and, both here and in Milano's subsequent involvement with #KeepTellingPeople (Serisier 2018: 113–115), the speaking *is* the work which unites women whose experiences—as well as their understanding of those experiences and motivations for speaking out—are otherwise very different. Whilst the emotional work of online disclosure is a growing theme in feminist scholarship (e.g. Mendes et al. 2019), questions about whether speaking out is in itself a transformative political practice have concerned feminist activists and scholars for some time (e.g. Alcoff and Gray 1993; Armstrong 1996; Serisier 2018; Alcoff 2018) and remain highly relevant in relation to #MeToo.

These three stories therefore set up some of the central concerns of this chapter. I begin by situating the "silence breaking" of the #MeToo moment in relation to a longer history of feminist speak outs and the activism, research and theory which these speak outs generated. In addition to raising questions about speech and the collective, this also raises fundamental questions about knowledge in light both of the repeated claims that "everybody knew" about Weinstein's behaviour, and the ahistorical media representations of #MeToo which divorce the hashtag from feminist knowledge, activism and research. I then move on to consider online affordances: how do these stories gain traction on and through social media? In the final section, I return to legacy media to explore how commentators have tried to make sense of this explosion of sexual harassment discourse on and offline. Central to this section is a concern with how these contemporary speak outs are—or are not—understood in relation to this longer history of feminism. This section thus presents original research which maps the discursive construction of feminism in, and in relation to, the Weinstein story at selected points in its development.

Speaking Out

Personal stories about rape and other forms of sexual violence are the foundation on which feminist theory and activism to end men's violence against women are built. As Tanya Serisier (2018: 4) notes in her impressive account of feminism, rape and narrative politics:

> feminist anti-rape politics is founded on the belief that producing and disseminating a genre of personal experiential narratives can end sexual violence. It is a belief, in the words of the well-known slogan, that "breaking the silence" through telling personal stories can and will "end the violence".

As Serisier acknowledges, the feminist project of speaking out is not an end in itself, rather it is a step towards challenging, and ultimately ending, men's violence against women. But for speech to have an impact, it has to be heard. It was through telling stories of their own experiences *and* listening to those of other women—in consciousness-raising groups and larger "speak outs"—that feminists were able to understand the common structure of their experiences. This understanding allowed them to build an analysis of sexual and other forms of men's violence, as well as to develop strategies to support women and challenge that violence.

The history of the feminist anti-rape movements in the US (Bevacqua 2000: 18–65) as well as similar movements in the UK (e.g. Maitland 2009; Browne 2014: 140–177; Scottish Women's Aid 2017) is thus intimately bound up with the process of speaking out and consciousness-raising. These and other feminist anti-violence movements broke the silence decades ago. In this sense, the #MeToo moment with its outpouring of victim/survivor testimony is not new; yet, this longer history of feminist speech is largely absent from popular understandings of #MeToo (as detailed in the final section). If the feminist past is not readily accessible, and feminist organisations in the present are struggling to maintain profile as well as funding, then it is hardly surprising if we seem to be reinventing the wheel. This is not simply about telling the same, or similar, stories again, but rather about divorcing these stories from the work of activist and advocacy organisations founded during the second wave whose work continues in the #MeToo moment. This creates schisms rather than connections with feminism's knowledge base, creating conditions for generational conflict to flourish.

It is worth pausing on the term consciousness-raising to consider its relationship to speaking out. Whilst speaking out assumes the primacy of experience, consciousness-raising suggests that a feminist understanding of that experience has to be built. This might be about naming or making public experiences which had previously been unspeakable or invisible. But it can also be about re-interpreting experiences which have long had a public character but have been understood only from a male point-of-view. This can mean making visible *as violence* experiences which have not previously been understood in this way. An obvious example here would be rape within marriage, which only became illegal in England and Wales in 1991, and Scotland in 1989, a husband's "right" to his wife's body having previously over-ridden her right to bodily autonomy. Nor is this an entirely historical curiosity: as I write, in March 2019, Mr Justice Hayden has spoken in court of the "fundamental human right" of a man to have sex with his wife (Bowcott 2019). That said, violence does not have to be recognisably criminal for it to contribute to gender inequality, nor has feminist theory or activism concentrated solely on criminal justice.

This intertwining of speech with process is encapsulated in a history project marking the 40th anniversary of Scottish Women's Aid—entitled, appropriately enough, *Speaking Out*. In the anniversary publication, we are told:

> Ultimately, Women's Aid in Scotland aims to "break the silence"—to raise awareness of domestic abuse among the public and policy makers, to change attitudes and promote women's equality and children's rights, to campaign for responses which actively prevent violence against women, and to bring an end to domestic abuse altogether. (Scottish Women's Aid 2017: 6)

Thus, speech is not an aim *in itself*, but rather a necessary precursor of the different kinds of work necessary to bring an end to domestic abuse. This suggests the ongoing centrality of victim/survivor experience to the movement, and also highlights the expertise within the organisation itself, built from decades of speaking, listening and acting. There are echoes here with Burke's (2018) argument that speaking out creates the conditions for the work, but is not, or not always, the work in itself.

Work is an important word in relation to consciousness-raising as it helps us to understand the commitment and organisation it required (e.g. Women's Liberation Workshop 1971/72). This work was typically conducted in small, women-only groups and the work of these groups was not only emotional, but also organisational, practical and theoretical (Hanisch 2010). Consciousness-raising demanded a considerable commitment of time and energy and was central to feminist theorising and activism in both the UK and the US (Megarry 2018a; Bevacqua 2000). As Jalna Hanmer put it, the consciousness-raising groups *were* the movement.[1]

In the US in particular, larger speak outs were also an important building block for activism and attracted wider public attention (Brownmiller 1975/1986; Armstrong 1987, 1996; Bevacqua 2000: 54–57). Whilst these made different demands on participants (not least in terms of the longevity of commitment), what the consciousness-raising groups and speak outs shared was the political use to which they put personal narratives, encapsulated in the second-wave slogan "the personal is political". Speak outs, conferences and movement publications provided some of the spaces for developing and sharing insights beyond the small group (Beins 2017; McKinney 2015; Bevacqua 2000), but as Megarry (2018a, b) argues, the closed nature of the groups was important in creating a space where women could develop an analysis free from male surveillance, something which she argues is missing from feminist attempts to build solidarity in digital networks. However, it is also important to note that consciousness-raising did not remain enclosed within the movement, but rather led to outward-facing activities from protests and campaigns to the establishment of services, and (sometimes fraught) attempts to engage with mainstream institutions, including the media (Dow 2014).

I want to turn here to Louise Armstrong's reflections on what this mass mediation did to the movement, specifically, in her case, the incest survivors' movement. Armstrong's book *Kiss Daddy Goodnight*—published in 1978—was modelled on the speak out, placing her own experiences alongside those of other women although, as Serisier (2018: 188–189) notes, Armstrong's narrative is deliberately selective and fails to account for race and class. Both in the Introduction to the tenth anniversary re-printing of *Kiss Daddy Goodnight* (Armstrong 1987) and subsequently in *Rocking the Cradle of Sexual Politics: What Happened When Women Said Incest* (1996), Armstrong reflects on the gap between what she intended speaking out to achieve and what happened next:

> "Well", people say to me, "But at least we're talking about it now."
>
> Yes. But it was not our intention merely to start a long conversation. Nor did we intend simply to offer up one more topic for talk shows, or one more plot option for ongoing dramatic series. We hoped to raise hell. We hoped to raise change. What we raised, it would seem, was discourse. And a sizable problem-management industry. Apart from protective service workers, we have researchers, family treatment programs, prevention experts, incest educators....It was not in our minds, either, ten years ago, that incest would become a career option.
>
> It in no way impugns the motives of those professionals who are dedicated to helping victims and survivors to suggest that the institutionalization of the problem does not augur its solution. (Armstrong 1987: ix)

Specifically, Armstrong is critically reflective of how the media engaged with "the World's First Walking, Talking Incest Victim", as she ironically labels herself (1996: 2). For the media, she argues, making this story public was the beginning and end of the narrative: speaking out became an end in itself, the personal is the public (Armstrong 1996: 3).

This publicising of the personal is embedded in the #MeToo moment, establishing an imperative to speak out which may not always benefit victim/survivors. Since the Weinstein story broke, women who have any kind of public profile have been routinely asked invasive questions about their own experiences and their thoughts on other women speaking out. For instance, as #MeToo spread to the Scottish political arena, female politicians were asked directly in live television interviews whether they had experienced sexual harassment (Aitken 2017). In this kind of questioning, the personal experiences of women who have a public role are assumed to be fair game for political reporters, usurping women's authority over the contexts of disclosure. In the UK at least, the media are not allowed to identify victims of sex crime unless they are given permission by the person involved; yet, here, establishing an imperative to speak out seems to have over-ridden these concerns.

Of course, this has not just been a feature of political reporting in the #MeToo era. Given the prominence of the Weinstein story, it is not surprising that sexual harassment became an almost routine line of questioning—particularly, though not exclusively, for women—in entertainment reporting in late 2017. This created some troubling dissonances, most famously perhaps in actor Uma Thurman's response to the sexual harassment question in a red carpet interview with *Access Hollywood*. In, politely, refusing the question, Thurman responded:

> I don't have a tidy soundbite for you, because I've learned – I'm not a child, and I've learned that when I've spoken in anger I usually regret the way I express myself. So I've been waiting to feel less angry. And when I'm ready, I'll say what I have to say. (Thurman, in Evans 2017)

This short interview, which went viral, is significant for my argument here for a number of reasons. As in the interviews with politicians, there is the sense that the public has a claim on Thurman's personal experience. Interviewed outside a theatre where she had begun previews for her debut Broadway performance, the line of questioning arguably constitutes a form of harassment in itself: here is a woman whose job requires that she engage with the media, being asked not about her professional role but rather about sexualised and traumatic personal experiences. And she has to play nice. As Soraya Chemaly (2018: 196–197) notes, Thurman made visible the tone policing she had to perform in that moment and her keen awareness of the precariousness of her position and how her emotions can be (and had been) used against her, despite her relative privilege in terms of race, profession and wealth (Orgad and Gill 2019).

Whilst the dynamics of disclosure in the #MeToo moment will have been different for women with a less public platform, nonetheless the imperative to speak out, to make the personal public, finds echoes in the accounts of women's decisions (not) to share #MeToo, or previous hashtags of disclosure (Mendes et al. 2019; Fileborn 2019). Armstrong's experience points to the way in which noise can perform a similar function to silence, in the way the media engages with women's experiences of male violence: distracting, diverting, distorting, disenfranchising (also Serisier 2018). In an analysis which has clear parallels with the way a number of celebrity abuse stories have unfolded, Armstrong notes that when stories of child sexual abuse were, finally, believed, they were recast as common sense, something that everybody (in particular, non-abusing mothers) knew. If everybody knew, then the responsibility was no longer with the perpetrator alone, and this had concrete repercussions for non-abusing mothers and their relationships with their children. As I will explore in Chap. 4, questions about the broader cultural investment in these narratives are important ones. At the same time, this wider cultural complicity can be quickly gendered so that women's knowledge (or failure to know) is what is at stake: as discussed in the interviews above. This is true not only in relation to women who could (or should) have witnessed, but also in relation to victim/survivors themselves. If everyone knew about Weinstein, then why did she go into a hotel room alone with him? The imperative to speak out is thus curiously linked to the assumption that everybody *already* knows.

The rationale for "keeping telling people" (to paraphrase the Creative Coalition's post #MeToo campaign on speaking out) lays responsibility for ending men's violence at the feet of victim/survivors and witnesses. Yet, the stories which mainstream media want to tell about these personal experiences are, as Armstrong also notes (1996: 38), personal ones. Without a feminist analysis (a feminist consciousness), the personal *remains* personal, as speaking publicly is constructed as part of a personally therapeutic process. This is in sharp contrast to the political character of consciousness-raising which was antithetical to therapy: consciousness-raising does not see the victim/survivor as the problem which needs to be fixed rather it ascribes this role to society (Armstrong 1996: 11). This is significant for an understanding of the #MeToo moment as it demands that we think critically about what it means to tell personal stories in a highly mediated context and invites us to think not only about who benefits from these tellings but also who has the opportunity to be heard and in what capacity.

Breaking the silence only gets us so far. For the stories to have political potential a first—but by no means sufficient—condition is to be able to link women's stories in a *collective* telling. As we will see, the affordances of social media extend the possibilities of these links, potentially globally. At the same time, some critics are cautious about the political potential of social media platforms in general and "hashtag feminism" has become the focus of considerable scholarly attention. It is to the debates raised in this work and the implications for how we might think of both the Weinstein case and #MeToo that I now turn my attention.

Speaking Out Online

How feminism operates in digital spaces is the focus of a growing scholarly literature (e.g. Fotopoulou 2016; Mendes et al. 2019). For some critics, it is feminism's embeddedness in everyday digital spaces—"in the very midst of the workings of current popular and digital culture" (Trakilovic cited in

Rentschler and Thrift 2015: 331)—which is its greatest potential, creating an open-access feminism which brings people to the movement, sometimes for the first time (Mendes et al. 2019; Blevins 2018; Desborough 2018). This has been particularly important for communities often marginalised *within* feminist movements and there is a growing literature on the potential of the digital for Black feminist organising in particular (Loza 2015; Conley 2017; Jackson 2016; Jackson et al. 2019).

In contrast, Megarry (2018a, b) is pessimistic about the potential of social media to replicate consciousness-raising groups, specifically because social media interactions take place under male surveillance. Differential access and digital literacy also generate and sustain divisions between feminists, particularly generational ones (Fotopoulou 2016: 44–47), whilst the necessity of maintaining a digital presence is even more challenging for feminist organisations facing funding cuts and increased precarity (ibid., 39, 54).

The digital has created new possibilities for those perpetuating sexual and gender-based violence and harassment as well as for those resisting it (Powell and Henry 2017; McGlynn et al. 2017). Indeed, scholars have documented the relatively routine experiences of gendered, sexualised and racialised abuse in online spaces (Megarry 2014; Mantilla 2015; Jane 2017; Vickery and Everbach 2018) and/or using digital technologies (Powell and Henry 2017; McGlynn et al. 2017; Powell et al. 2018), compounding the sense that the inequities of the digital world are an extension of what those women, and particularly minority women, experience offline.

It is therefore not surprising that what this means for feminists who use online spaces to challenge men's violence has been a topic of recurring concern. In particular, there has been an interest in online disclosures of sexual and other forms of gendered violence, including under previous hashtags such as #BeenRapedNeverReported (Mendes et al. 2019: 125–144), #YesAllWomen (Serisier 2018: 93–116; Jackson et al. 2019; Jackson and Banaszczyk 2016), #SayHerName (Williams 2016), #IAmNotAfraidToSayIt (Lokot 2018), as well as through online campaigns, including Everyday Sexism, Hollaback! and Harassmap (Mendes et al. 2019; Fileborn 2014, 2017; Powell and Henry 2017; Skalli 2014). These studies point to the ways in which personal experiences are linked with hashtags to become part of a curated conversation. Whilst individual users cannot control how that conversation develops, disclosures of sexual violence are read relationally. Women's motivations for disclosing are revealed in these studies to variously include the importance of being heard and believed (often for the first time) through "peer-to-peer witnessing" (Loney-Howes 2018); affective solidarity (Mendes et al. 2019: 125–144); advice-seeking (O'Neill 2018); and disclosure as exposure, awareness raising or educating others (Skalli 2014; Mendes et al. 2019: 100–124; Crawley and Simic 2018). This scholarship also explores the role of online disclosure in "new social practices of informal justice in response to rape" (Powell 2015: 572), particularly where criminal justice is not open to women, or has failed (Salter 2013; Fileborn 2017; Mohammed 2019). Whilst some women describe the relative "safety" of specific platforms as spaces of disclosure, "the ability to harness and reap the benefits of online disclosure is largely uneven" (Mendes et al. 2019: 67), not least because of the emotional labour involved and the potential of abusive responses, which can themselves replicate elements of the original experience of abuse, harassment or discrimination in ways that are gendered, sexualised and racialised. This produces sometimes contradictory affective engagements, encapsulated in the subtitle of Aristea Fotopoulou's book on *Feminist Activism and Digital Networks: Between Empowerment and Vulnerability* (2016).

Serisier's (2018) work also asks important questions about who is heard on social media and which voices are amplified. This demonstrates the impossibility of thinking of the affordances of social media in isolation, as there is an inextricable link between social media and legacy media, which means some voices are amplified more than others (Alcoff 2018). Recent writing has raised important questions around how women's work—and the work of Black and other women of colour in particular—is co-opted (Serisier 2018: 93–116; Jackson et al. 2019), often without credit (Bailey and Trudy 2018; Loza 2015: 7; Garza 2014). This reflects existing power structures, but is also enabled by the platforms themselves which privilege decontextualised forms of communication.

For instance, the story of #YesAllWomen—a hashtag started by Muslim feminist Kaye M in response to #NotAllMen—reveals processes of co-option, whitewashing and abuse, as well as solidarity and political engagement (Serisier 2018; Kaye M 2015). Serisier and Kaye M detail how, for some white feminists, the intersectional demand of Kaye M's #YesAllWomen was a distraction from a gendered analysis, so that rather than amplifying Kaye M's message, they co-opted it, and even attacked its originator. At the same time, Kaye M faced a racialised misogynist backlash. Kaye M's own account of this period (2015) reveals the emotional costs of #YesAllWomen both in terms of bearing witness to the accounts of abuse women shared using the hashtag and in terms of her sudden hypervisibility and the equally sudden (and swift) personal threat this engendered.

Kaye M's account is a cautionary one in terms of the hidden costs of the economy of visibility where people posting in a personal capacity have no institutional support or resources to deal with a racialised, gendered backlash on a platform which is notoriously ineffectual in policing racialised, gendered threats. The emotional labour and vulnerability to abuse involved in being online—particularly for women of colour—is increasingly recognised in the literature (Loza 2015; Hackworth 2018; Madden et al. 2018), and, as Kaye M's account demonstrates, this places significant restrictions on the potential of activist engagement with the platform. The lack of gatekeepers for a platform like Twitter means that it has a certain democratic potential, particularly when juxtaposed with the institutional biases of mainstream media (Williams 2015, 2016). Yet, when marginalised voices do achieve the prominence promised by the democratic mythology of the platform, they do so without the institutional support or material advantage that those speaking from more secure positions may enjoy (Bailey and Trudy 2018). I certainly do not want to overstate the potential of institutional support here: many institutions which require and profit from their employees' social media use have yet to take responsibility for the different ways this impacts on women and other marginalised employees (Everbach 2018; Jane 2018; Gardiner 2018; Olson and LaPoe 2018; Savigny 2019; Vera-Gray 2017). Moreover, the increasing precarity of labour—particularly, but by no means exclusively, in media and cultural industries—means that fewer and fewer workers enjoy labour protections of this kind (Jane 2018). Nevertheless, dealing with a social media pile on as an individual, as Kaye M describes, is a very different experience than dealing with such a pile on when you are, notionally at least, speaking on behalf of an organisation, as women who have experienced both suggest.[2]

Questions around acknowledgement, ownership, leadership and community also arise in Tarana Burke's reflections on #MeToo. As Burke notes, thanks to the interventions of Black women online, her activism has now become part of the mainstream narrative around #MeToo,[3] and her leadership is also widely recognised within online feminist networks (Xiong et al. 2019: 16). Yet, she has also reflected on the roles she has been cast in by mainstream media:

While it's true that I have been widely recognized as the "founder" of the movement – there is virtually no mention of my leadership. Like I just discovered something 12 years ago and in 2017 it suddenly gained value. #metooMVMT #metoo (@TaranaBurke, 21 February 2018)

What is at stake in these representations is therefore not her breaking of the silence (in 2007), but rather the amplification of her message through its celebrification and extension beyond the group of Black and brown girls who have long been the primary focus of Burke's work. Burke's experience highlights the ways in which an increased mainstream profile can come at the cost of the flattening out of the intersectional specificities and demands of the work. She describes this as being "acknowledged and erased", as mainstream media both gives voice to survivors whilst distorting their analysis and restricting their authority (Serisier 2018: 102; Armstrong 1996; Alcoff and Gray 1993). Burke's account suggests that "the work" gets lost in accounts which seize on the *person* of the "founder" rather than the continuing *activism* of a "leader": a tension which other scholars have similarly observed in the translation of online campaigns to mainstream media texts (Darmon 2014).

One of the key tensions I want to get at here, then, is that whilst the affordances of social media enable connection, these are easily decontextualised. This facilitates the misremembering of feminism's pasts in the wider discourses social media users participate in, particularly as this relates to the long-standing contributions and challenges of feminists of colour (Collins and Bilge 2016: 63–113; Loza 2015; Hemmings and Brain 2003). It is not only feminism's *pasts* which are erased here but also—importantly—the longevity of, and expertise acquired within, *ongoing* movements. Whilst high-profile activities such as the launch of TimesUp! *have* acknowledged and sought to support this ongoing work, as I will demonstrate in the next section, this has not typically been part of the mainstream media narrative.

WHAT'S FEMINISM GOT TO DO WITH IT?

The sexual harassment and assault story that began with the Weinstein articles in the *New York Times* and *New Yorker* is, in obvious ways, a story about gender inequality. Twohey, Kantor and Farrow's stories reveal Weinstein's systematic abuse of women over whom he held a degree of professional as well as physical power, as well as the structures within the industry which enabled his behaviour. In many ways, this was, from the outset, a story informed by a *feminist* analysis of sexual harassment in the context of gender inequality. However, mainstream understandings of the place of feminism in this story have been ambivalent and contradictory at best.

Time magazine's *Person of the Year* issue with which I opened this chapter is emblematic of these tensions.[4] This story engages with and reflects upon the feminist-informed process of speaking out, centring the experiences of survivors and connecting the experiences of the economically and racially privileged women of the entertainment industry with those of minority women whose economic status is more precarious. What unites these women (and two men)—Hollywood actors, strawberry pickers, hotel housekeepers, engineers, lobbyists—is their experience of workplace sexual harassment from men and the fact that they have spoken out about it, albeit with different degrees of publicity and anonymity.

In some ways, this is a quintessentially feminist story. Yet, feminism is an oblique presence in the article:

> Like the "problem that has no name", the disquieting malaise of frustration and repression among postwar wives and homemakers identified by Betty Friedan more than 50 years ago, this moment is born of a very real and potent sense of unrest. (Zacharek et al. 2017)

Friedan's *The Feminine Mystique* (1963) is widely understood to be foundational to the growth of white, liberal feminism in the US, though Friedan herself was critical of the focus on men's violence against women in much feminist activism in the years that followed (Bevacqua 2000: 6). The article provides this link to a very select white, liberal feminist past, divorcing #MeToo both from the specific history of feminist activism against men's violence and from an intersectional feminist present. Notably, the word "feminist" is used only twice and, as Serisier (2018: 93) also notes, it is associated with suspicion (feminists supported Bill Clinton despite sexual harassment allegations against him) or disavowal (the women coming forward do not see themselves as feminists). Moreover, whilst the article privileges the voices of survivors, the other experts it references specialise in social movements, workplace training and organisational psychology, *not* in men's violence against women or gender inequality. Although Tarana Burke is featured, the intersectional challenge of her Me Too movement is watered down to "a non-profit that *helps* survivors of sexual violence" and encourages "young women to show solidarity with one another" (Zacharek et al. 2017). Support for survivors is an important part of activist work. However, as discussed above, the feminist speak out tradition—in seeking to build a structural, political analysis and to change social reality—is at odds with a *purely* therapeutic tradition (Armstrong 1996: 11). Moreover, this reframing of Burke's work also undermines the expertise gathered from working *with* young women of colour, instead emphasising first-person survivor-testimony.

The *Time* story thus encapsulates the "double entanglement" which feminist cultural theorist Angela McRobbie (2009) argues has characterised mainstream media's engagements with feminism since the 1990s. Feminism is "taken into account" as the ground on which this story is built, at the same time that the contemporary relevance of feminism is disavowed. The #MeToo moment as represented in this *Time* story is one in which feminism is notably absent as a *continuing* presence, a body of *knowledge* and a social *movement*. It is the movement with no name, and thus no history.

"The Silence Breakers" is far from an isolated example of this "double entanglement". In the remainder of this chapter, I analyse news coverage of two key moments in the global sexual harassment story, working with a corpus of English-language news publications identified through searching the Nexis database for articles which use the words Weinstein *and* feminist *or* feminism. An initial search for the keyword combination in two key periods—October 2017 (when the Weinstein story broke and #MeToo first went viral) and January 2018 (which saw the launch of TimesUp!)—was refined through manual exclusion of duplicates and teasers to produce the final corpus of 638 stories. Although my analysis—based on close reading of the corpus—is qualitative,[5] it is worth noting at the outset that the link with feminism is made in a tiny, but growing, fraction of all the stories which mention Weinstein (244 of 16,928 in October 2017; 394 of 8088 in January 2018). In both periods, there are articles which are positive and unapologetic about the necessity of feminist analysis: the term "sexism" is fairly widely used; "gender inequality" is understood as the wider context for sexual harassment; and even terms like "rape culture" (Gay 2017), "patriarchy" (Allan 2017) and "intersectionality" (Garcia 2017) are used. Individual "feminists"—typically politicians and journalists—are occasionally cited, but notably these are not typically people with expertise on sexual harassment or other forms of men's violence against women. Instead, feminism is more typically a moralising opinion, a "hot take" on a controversial issue (Banet-Weiser 2018b), or, more sinisterly, a site of suspicion or barrier to progress.

The construction of feminism as a site of suspicion is there from the very beginning of the Weinstein story. Partly, this is a result of the central role played by lawyer, Weinstein's adviser, and "fake feminist"[6] Lisa Bloom who is prominently and strategically deployed in the first days after the publication of Twohey and Kantor's story to indicate Weinstein's willingness to change as well as to deny criminal wrongdoing. This pits Bloom against her mother, feminist lawyer Gloria Allred, who has represented a number of sexual assault survivors, including those (allegedly) assaulted by Donald Trump and Bill Cosby. The effect of this is twofold: firstly establishing feminism as a site of suspicion (something that can be faked by privileged women like Bloom), and secondly casting feminist disagreement as both interpersonal and intergenerational.

Bloom's involvement with Weinstein was relatively short-lived; however, she is not the only suspect feminist to appear—Hillary Clinton and Meryl Streep are also routinely characterised in this way. In these stories, their feminism is cast as hypocritical and opportunistic in light of their association with Weinstein and their failure to issue immediate public statements following the *New York Times* story. Such reports often take their cue from Rose McGowan's Twitter feed, demonstrating the inextricability of old and new platforms and the appeal of sexual assault stories which pit women against women, decentring perpetrators. This construction of feminism as hypocritical and opportunistic is reinforced by reference to Weinstein's own self-promotion as a feminist prior to October 2017, with many stories following the lead established by Kantor and Twohey in mentioning his acts of feminist "philanthropy" (the endowment of a Gloria Steinem Chair at Rutgers), support for feminist filmmaking (in particular *The Hunting Ground* [dir. Kirby Dick, 2015]), and participation in feminist protest (the 2017 Women's March at the Sundance Film Festival).

There are questions to be asked about the wider culture of complicity which supported Weinstein (which I return to in Chap. 4). However, what concerns me here is the way in which this emphasis on individual feminists is used to confirm the *failures* of feminism. Despite Clinton's and Streep's denials, there are repeated assertions that these women *must* have known such that their complicity becomes the story. The-taint-of-Weinstein attaches to these and other prominent women to become a convenient shorthand for dismissing their feminist activism, particularly in relation to challenging men's sexual violence. This extends beyond the periods studied. For instance, in other work conducted with Chamil Rathnayake (and discussed in Chap. 5), I found that Alyssa Milano's friendship with Weinstein and his wife was used by conservative critics on social media to discredit her activism with, and on behalf of, victim/survivors (Boyle and Rathnayake 2019). It is notable that this guilt-by-association has been much less vehemently maintained for the many men who benefitted from Weinstein's patronage even when—like Quentin Tarantino (Kantor 2017)—they have admitted that they *did* know enough to have done something about it.

Casting feminism as a site of suspicion also depends on feminism being equated with the behaviour of individual women who call themselves feminists. Whenever a woman in the public eye comments on Weinstein in a way that is deemed problematic, this becomes a battleground for the meaning of feminism and the right to call oneself a feminist. This is consistent with my argument that feminism is constructed as an opinion more often than a source of expertise, or indeed support.

My discussion thus far has focused on the first month of reporting (October 2017), a period characterised by near daily revelations against men in the screen industries, as well as by the explosion of survivor discourse following Milano's #MeToo tweet (15 October). Given that this is the beginning of the #MeToo moment, it is perhaps not surprising that an explicitly feminist analysis is relatively marginalised, but whilst feminism looms larger in the later period studied, it remains a contradictory presence. The first week of January is dominated by two stories: the importance of Weinstein and, relatedly, feminism to reviews of the year gone by; and the 1 January launch of TimesUp!, an initiative led by women in the entertainment industries to provide financial and legal support to women experiencing sexual harassment in other sectors. This heightened visibility of feminism—and specifically of feminist *action*—is nicely encapsulated in the *Washington Post*'s list predicting what is "in" and "out" in 2018, which signals a shift from feminism as an accessory (feminist tees are "out") to feminism in action (feminist lawmakers are "in") (Contrera and Mason 2018). It is fitting, then, that January also includes the second Women's March and numerous published reflections on the fallout from the Weinstein story and the implications for women of Trump's first year in office.

Much of the commentary generated by the launch of TimesUp! alongside the Golden Globes protest (where women dressed in black as a protest against sexual harassment in the industry, and Hollywood stars brought gender and racial justice activists with them to the ceremony), speaks to the continuing tensions in the construction of a popular, and celebrity-oriented, feminism. Whilst the coverage is not entirely support-ive—with critiques both from anti-feminist and some feminist positions—nevertheless much of the reporting is centrally *about* feminist issues and strategies. There is, for instance, considerable discussion about the possibilities and challenges of intersectional feminist politics and practice, and how, or whether, a movement led by economically and racially privileged actors can foster change. Interestingly, this moves beyond passing judgement on individual feminists (as in the first days of the Weinstein story), to think critically about activist practice.

The most insightful writing links women's experiences of sexual harassment with gender inequality, particularly in reporting on the Women's March where harassment is often discussed alongside other issues including employment, political representation and reproductive rights. There is also a greater use of spokespeople representing feminist and equality-based organisations, as well as feminist academics, although these experts tend to be deployed when feminism itself is the focus, as, for example, in stories about the legacies and futures of the Women's March and #MeToo. The activists who appeared on the Golden Globes red carpet are namechecked in a number of articles, though the coverage rarely extends much beyond the namecheck. Perhaps unsurprisingly, among the eight activists, only Me Too founder Tarana Burke and the Executive Director of Imkaan, Marai Larasi, focus specifically on men's (sexual) violence against women in their work. In a statement released through TimesUp!, the Golden Globes protest is presented as a reaction to perpetrator-oriented, non-intersectional press coverage, and an attempt to expand the conversation beyond Hollywood and connect the #MeToo moment to broader inequalities:

> "Too much of the recent press attention has been focused on perpetrators and does not adequately address the systematic nature of violence including the importance of race, ethnicity and economic status in sexual violence and other forms of violence against women."
>
> "Our goal in attending the Golden Globes is to shift the focus back to survivors and on systemic, lasting solutions [...] to broaden conversations about the connection to power, privilege and other systemic inequalities." (Chavez 2018)

In this context, the inclusion of (feminist) labour-rights, sports and environmental activists makes sense. Indeed, it was the statement of solidarity with women in Hollywood from Alianza Nacional de Campesinas—an organisation working on behalf of female farm-workers across the US—which initiated the cross-class solidarity which led to TimesUp! (TimesUp!, n.d.). The centring of these organisations thus underlines the point that sexual harassment is not the preserve of one sector or demographic.

However, this is not without contradictions. Firstly, it is notable that the reports which devote most space to the work of the organisations are also those which linger longest on the details of the women's appearance. The quotation above, for instance, is taken from an article on the *Daily Mail*'s TV & Showbiz pages which includes a lengthy description of Emma Stone's dress, make-up and hair, her make-up artist and hairstylist given more space than TimesUp! Moreover, the very collectivity and solidarity which TimesUp! centres on, allows the *specific* work of these women and their organisations to be widely ignored. This failure to tap into feminist *expertise*—even when so prominently on display—is notable.

The day after the Golden Globes, 100 French women including, most famously, actor Catherine Deneuve, signed a letter to *Le Monde* decrying the #MeToo moment as a "witch hunt", characterised by "puritanism", which "chains women to the status of eternal victim".[7] As we have already seen, the Weinstein story quickly became a battleground for the meaning of feminism, and by January 2018, this battle was routinely presented in generational and moralistic terms. Alongside Deneuve and her co-signatories, Daphne Merkin, in the *New York Times* (2018) claimed that "we seem to be returning to a victimology paradigm for young women", whilst Germaine Greer, in a much-reported comment, suggested that women had "spread their legs" for Weinstein to land movie roles. The ways in which the arguments of these women were taken up demonstrate the limitations of framing feminism as an individual quality (you are or are not a feminist) and an opinion (held by feminist individuals). Merkin, Greer, Deneuve and others are therefore constructed as *opposing* #MeToo, prompting online responses that are vitriolic and ageist, and themselves becoming the focus of extensive mainstream commentary. Actor Asia Argento, who went public about Weinstein in October 2017, suggested of Deneuve and her co-signatories that "their interiorized misogyny has lobotomized them to the point of no return" (McKay 2018), while Katie Way—whose article on Aziz Ansari I will return to—described TV-anchor Ashleigh Banfield as a "burgundy-lipstick, bad-highlights, second-wave feminist" in a message which Banfield read on air.[8] This is feminism as a generational catfight—or "intergenerational feminist soap opera" (Rivers 2017: 42–43)—rather than as a movement where, by definition, there must be disagreement, dialogue and development. Moreover, this is a catfight which profits the media platforms which stoke it, and provides free—or cheap—content for legacy media by extracting value from women's words. As Moira Weigel (2018) argues, women and other marginalised groups may have louder voices in social media than legacy media, but they are not the ones making money from the stories their words generate.

In the construction of Deneuve, Merkin and Greer as relics of a bygone era, there are uncomfortable echoes of Weinstein's attempt to recast the Kantor and Twohey story as evidence of a generational culture-clash. In lieu of an apology, in a statement to the *New York Times* Weinstein noted that he came of age in the 1960s and 1970s "when all the rules about behaviour and workplaces were different" (Weinstein 2017). Of course, Weinstein's memory is self-servingly selective, writing out the rise of feminism in those decades. However, if Deneuve, Merkin or Greer serves as a stand-in for the feminist 1970s, second-wave feminism can be presented as part of the problem that contemporary women are revolting against. The fact that the feminist 1970s saw the founding of women's refuge and rape crisis movements—movements which continue to this day—is neatly obscured, as is the possibility of feminist *expertise*, derived, for instance, from decades of research or direct work with victim/survivors. A telling comparison here is with the treatment of poet and playwright Liz Lochhead's claim that Scottish poet Robert Burns was the Weinstein of his day. In debating Burns' legacy, articles in Scottish press drew heavily on recognised academic experts on Burns as well as on evidence of Burns' influence on contemporary literary figures (Morrison 2018; Williams 2018). It would seem that literary criticism requires an expertise that understanding men's violence against women does not.

Also in January 2018, Babe.net published a story about a "bad date" with comedian Aziz Ansari in which a young woman, pseudonymously referred to as "Grace", recounts a night with the actor which left her feeling "violated" after he "ignored clear non-verbal cues" (Way 2018). This story generated considerable mainstream coverage and was often part of a broader conversation about whether #MeToo has gone too far. It is notable, however, that these stories are typically opinion pieces, and whilst these often make use of a feminist language around meaningful consent, power and sexual pleasure, the genre of opinion writing privileges personal morality and judgement. Ansari's publicly *feminist* persona prior to the

Babe story is also important: if Ansari (like Weinstein) can also present himself as a feminist, then this justifies the suspicion of feminism as a self-serving ideology which circulates in mainstream media discourse. When everyone is, or can be a feminist, feminist knowledge—built from experience, activism and research—is rendered largely irrelevant.

Reflecting on media requests received by Scottish feminist organisation Engender in the first days after #MeToo went viral, Alys Mumford (2017) noted this tendency of media organisations to frame the debate around conflict and, specifically, the authenticity and believability of women. This not only personalises the issue and promotes victim blaming, but also means that many feminist organisations cannot and will not take part in these debates because they are based on a false premise. I have heard from other colleagues in feminist organisations that their media requests peaked when the story could be framed as a question as to whether #MeToo had "gone too far". In other words, the media does not draw on these organisations' decades of experience working with women, but rather aims to construct a debate about men's "victimisation", a theme I return to in Chap. 5.

Of course, it is possible—and perhaps even strategically desirable at times—to do feminist work without using the word "feminism". I was curious to establish whether organisations working against sexual violence were more widely represented than my initial searches suggested. So, I conducted a further search for Weinstein stories which mentioned either the Rape, Abuse and Incest National Network (RAINN) (the largest anti-sexual violence organisation in the US) or rape crisis (a term used fairly internationally by feminist organisations). Of the nearly 17,000 stories on the Nexis database mentioning Weinstein in October 2017, only 82 articles mention these leading organisations, and this is even more marked in January, where there are only 28 mentions (in 8810 stories). Notably, 20% of these stories[9] are about prominent figures making guilt-money donations to offset the way they have profited from their connections with Weinstein or Woody Allen. Very few stories make use of experts from these or other specialist organisations working on sexual harassment or abuse and, although the numbers are too small to be anything other than suggestive, spokespeople from organisations working to challenge perpetrators or support victim/survivors seem more likely to be used in publications which have a smaller geographical reach. A headline in *The Sentinel*—a publication based in Carlisle, Pennsylvania—encapsulates this nicely when it notes "National focus on harassment sparks local discussions" (Gitt

2018). Student newspapers are also over-represented in the Weinstein *and* RAINN/rape crisis dataset (19 of 82 reports are from university publications). This might suggest cause for optimism in the next generation of journalists, but it also reaffirms the fact that mainstream English-language news outlets made little use of the expertise of the feminist anti-violence sector in reporting the sexual assault and rape allegations against Weinstein.

Although good practice guidelines for responsible reporting of men's violence against women suggest signposting to support organisations (Zero Tolerance 2018; NUJ 2013), my initial searches for Weinstein and feminism/feminist produced not a single direct reference to sources of support, and only 17 stories (of 110) in the RAINN/rape crisis corpus included helplines or other links to support. Interestingly, if surprisingly, these were primarily in the context of celebrity and entertainment rather than news. The only publications to list helplines on more than one occasion were *Hollywood Life* (an online entertainment magazine) and *New Musical Express* (a UK print-based publication), with three each. Whilst these numbers are too small for robust conclusions, this nonetheless highlights the relative marginalisation of feminist expertise, at the same time pointing to the importance of celebrity and entertainment journalism for feminist scholars interested in the reporting of male violence against women.

This analysis therefore reveals something of the messiness of the discursive construction of feminism in relation to the Weinstein case, echoing McRobbie's arguments about the "double entanglement" whereby feminism is that which is taken into account in order to be moved beyond. Admittedly, feminism is now considerably more popular than when McRobbie was writing a decade ago (Banet-Weiser 2018a), and I found many articles which were forthright in their feminist analysis. Indeed, the kind of analysis I have presented has echoes in newspaper articles which provide a meta-commentary on the position of feminism in media reporting (e.g. Bennett 2018; Funnell 2018). What my analysis adds to these accounts is evidence of the continued marginalisation of feminist activists, organisations and researchers who could put these arguments in broader, evidence-based contexts. To the extent that feminism thrives in mainstream contexts, it is as an individual opinion which also makes it open to personalised rebuke. This has implications for individual victim/survivors who bear the emotional weight of the #MeToo narrative, whether or not their accounts are picked up beyond their immediate circle (Mendes et al. 2019).

Conclusion

The principle of the feminist speak outs was to give personal stories a political character through understanding their commonalities with other personal stories. At one level, #MeToo has been phenomenally successful in achieving this and I do not want to downplay either the personal bravery or the political importance of the leaders of this movement or of the individual women and men who have disclosed (and continue to disclose) their experiences in this context. However, as Jessica Megarry argues (2018a, b), the indiscriminate audience for a social media status means that the act of speaking out is—in some ways—divorced from the intellectual, political and organisational work, the commitment of time and energy involved in listening as well as speaking, which feminist consciousness-raising demanded. As these stories migrate from social media to mainstream media, women's control of their narratives is limited and the stories depoliticised. Feminism is no longer the movement which gives rise to these disclosures, supports women and develops knowledge, policy and analysis, but is recast as a moralising opinion, a hot take (Banet-Weiser 2018b). This decontextualisation allows for the feminist story of sexual harassment and violence in the context of gender inequality to be recast as a story about feminist (and feminists') in-fighting. Whilst personal silences are broken, political silences can be paradoxically reinforced.

Notes

1. Transcript and audio of excerpts of 2010 oral history with Jalna Hanmer for the Sisterhood and After project, available at: https://www.bl.uk/collection-items/jalna-hanmer-consciousness-raising-groups
2. This argument is indebted to panellists at the "Violence Unseen" discussion which I chaired at the University of Strathclyde, 25 March 2019: Lily Greenan, Brenna Jessie, Claire Heuchan and Anni Donaldson. See also Mendes et al. (2019: 88–89).
3. See, in particular, a thread @TaranaBurke posted 15 October 2018 (https://twitter.com/taranaburke/status/1051840689477246978?lang=en)
4. Catherine Mayer, co-founder of the Women's Equality Party in the UK, reveals an additional contradiction in *Time*'s championing of the "silence breakers". Also in 2017, Mayer brought a sex and age discrimination case against *Time* (Mayer 2018). That "the traffic in feminism" (Banet-Weiser and Portwood-Stacer 2017) can be profitable for the very mainstream media companies which feminists might rally against in other contexts is one of the central contradictions of the current climate (Mendes et al. 2019: 31).

5. Following the approach I adopted in a previous project which maps the development of the Jimmy Savile sexual abuse news story (Boyle 2018), this stage of the research deployed a qualitative, inductive approach to the material based on close reading. This allowed me to chart the development of the Weinstein story, noting both the language used to describe claims at different stages in the story and the role feminism—and feminists—played in the telling of these stories. It is worth noting here that the total corpus of 638 stories amounted to literally thousands of pages of text: very few of the articles were short news items; most were longer opinion pieces and the corpus also includes a number of transcripts from current affairs programmes on US television. My intent in this chapter is to note patterns in the coverage which I hope will prove suggestive for future research examining the discursive construction of feminism in the reporting of feminist issues in mainstream media.

6. Bloom is dubbed a "fake feminist" repeatedly on Fox News' *Tucker Carlson Tonight*. See, for example, the broadcasts on 18 October, 21 October, 27 October and 28 October, all available on the Nexis database.

7. A full English translation of the letter can be found here https://www. worldcrunch.com/opinion-analysis/full-translation-of-french-anti-metoo-manifesto-signed-by-catherine-deneuve. Accessed 20 May 2019.

8. *Primetime Justice with Ashleigh Banfield*, CNN, 16 January 2018.

9. N = 22, with 8 stories in October, and 14 in January following this pattern.

REFERENCES

Aitken, Mark. 2017. BBC refuse to apologise to MSP for grilling her over harassment on live TV. *Daily Record*, 5 November. https://www.dailyrecord. co.uk/news/scottish-news/bbc-refuse-say-sorry-msp-11469567. Accessed 3 April 2019.

Alcoff, Linda Martín. 2018. *Rape and Resistance: Understanding the Complexities of Sexual Violation*. Cambridge & Medford: Polity.

Alcoff, Linda Martín and Laura Gray. 1993. Survivor discourse: transgression or recuperation. *Signs* 18 (2): 260–290.

Allan, Drew. 2017. We must strive to overcome this world of boorish excess. *The Herald* (Glasgow), 17 October.

Armstrong, Louise. 1987. *Kiss Daddy Goodnight: Ten Years Later*. New York: Pocket Books.

Armstrong, Louise. 1996. *Rocking the Cradle of Sexual Politics: What Happened When Women Said Incest*. London: The Women's Press.

Bailey, Moya and Trudy. 2018. On misogynoir: citation, erasure, and plagiarism. *Feminist Media Studies* 18 (4): 762–768.

Banet-Weiser, Sarah. 2018a. *Empowered: Popular Feminism and Popular Misogyny.* Durham, NC: Duke University Press.

Banet-Weiser, Sarah. 2018b. Popular feminism: feminist flashpoints. *LA Review of Books,* 5 October. https://lareviewofbooks.org/article/popular-feminism-feminist-flashpoints/#! Accessed 1 April 2019.

Banet-Weiser, Sarah and Laura Portwood-Stacer. 2017. The traffic in feminism. *Feminist Media Studies* 7 (5): 884–888,

Beins, Agatha. 2017. *Liberation in Print: Feminist Periodicals and Social Movement Identity.* Athens: University of Georgia Press.

Bennett, Catherine. 2018. When feminists insult each other chauvinists cheer. *The Observer,* 28 January.

Bevacqua, Maria. 2000. *Rape on the Public Agenda: Feminism and the Politics of Sexual Assault.* Richmond: Northeastern University Press.

Blevins, Katie. 2018. bell hooks and consciousness-raising: argument for a fourth wave of feminism. In *Mediating Misogyny: Gender, Technology & Harassment,* ed. Jacqueline Vickery and Tracy Everbach, 91–108. Cham: Palgrave Macmillan.

Bowcott, Owen. 2019. English judge says man having sex with wife is "fundamental human right". *Guardian,* 3 April.

Boyle, Karen. 2018. Hiding in plain sight: gender, sexism and press coverage of the Jimmy Savile case. *Journalism Studies* 19 (11): 1562–1578.

Boyle, Karen and Chamil Rathnayake. 2019. #HimToo and the networking of misogyny in the age of #MeToo. *Feminist Media Studies.* DOI: https://doi.org/10.1080/14680777.2019.1661868.

Browne, Sarah. 2014. *The Women's Liberation Movement in Scotland.* Manchester: Manchester University Press.

Brownmiller, Susan. 1975/1986. *Against Our Will: Men, Women, and Rape.* London: Pelican Books.

Burke, Tarana. 2018. Me Too is a movement, not a moment. Ted Talk, November. https://www.ted.com/talks/tarana_burke_me_too_is_a_movement_not_a_moment. Accessed 22 January 2019.

Burke, Tarana (n.d.) The Inception. *Me Too,* https://metoomvmt.org/the-inception/. Accessed 2 April 2019.

Chavez, Paul. 2018. She's ace: Emma Stone brings Billie Jean King to Golden Globes after nomination for playing tennis icon, *DailyMail.Com,* 8 January. https://www.dailymail.co.uk/tvshowbiz/article-5245045/Emma-Stone-brings-Billie-Jean-King-Golden-Globe-Awards.html. Accessed 12 April.

Chemaly, Soraya. 2018. *Rage Becomes Her: The Power of Women's Anger.* London & New York: Simon and Schuster.

Collins, Patricia Hill and Sirma Bilge. 2016. *Intersectionality.* Cambridge: Polity.

Conley, Tara L. 2017. Decoding black feminist hashtags as becoming. *The Black Scholar* 47 (3): 22–32.

Contrera, Jessica and Everdeen Mason. 2018. The list 2018. *Washington Post*, 1 January.

Crawley, Karen and Olivera Simic. 2018. Telling stories of rape, revenge and redemption in the age of the TED talk. *Crime, Media, Culture* DOI: https://doi.org/10.1177/1741659018771117.

Darmon, Keren. 2014. Framing SlutWalk London: how does the privilege of feminist activism in social media travel into the mass media? *Feminist Media Studies* 14(4): 700–704.

Desborough, Karen. 2018. The global anti-street harassment movement: digitally-enabled feminist activism. In *Mediating Misogyny: Gender, Technology & Harassment*, eds. Jacqueline Vickery and Tracy Everbach, 333–351. Cham: Palgrave Macmillan.

Dow, Bonnie J. 2014. *Watching Women's Liberation 1970: Feminism's Pivotal Year on the Network News*. Urbana, Chicago, Springfield: University of Illinois Press.

Evans, Greg. 2017. Uma Thurman on sexual harassment: "when I'm ready, I'll say what I have to say". *Deadline Hollywood*, 4 November. https://deadline.com/2017/11/uma-thurman-access-hollywood-sexual-harassment-harvey-weinstein-1202201978/ Accessed 3 April 2019.

Everbach, Tracy. 2018. 'I realized it was about them....not me': women sports journalists and harassment. In *Mediating Misogyny: Gender, Technology & Harassment*, eds. Jacqueline Vickery and Tracy Everbach, 131–149. Cham: Palgrave Macmillan.

Farrow, Ronan. 2017a. From aggressive overtures to sexual assault: Harvey Weinstein's accusers tell their stories. *The New Yorker*, 10 October.

Farrow, Ronan. 2017b. Harvey Weinstein's army of spies. *The New Yorker*, 6 November.

Felsenthal, Edward. 2017. The choice. *Time*, December.

Fileborn, Bianca. 2014. Online activism and street harassment: Digital justice or shouting into the ether? *Griffith Journal of Law and Human Dignity* 2 (1): 32–51.

Fileborn, Bianca. 2017. Justice 2.0: street harassment victims' use of social media and online activism and sites of informal justice. *British Journal of Criminology* 57: 1482–1501.

Fileborn, Bianca. 2019. Naming the unspeakable harm of street harassment: a survey-based examination of disclosure practices. *Violence Against Women* 25 (2): 223–248.

Fotopoulou, Aristea. 2016. *Feminist Activism and Digital Networks: Between Empowerment and Vulnerability*. London: Palgrave Macmillan.

Friedan, Betty. 1963. *The Feminine Mystique*. New York: WW Norton & Co.

Funnell, Nina. 2018. Q&A what were you thinking? *The Age*, 25 January.

Garcia, Sandra E. 2017. The woman who created #MeToo long before hashtags. *New York Times*, 21 October.

Gardiner, Becky. 2018. "It's a terrible way to go to work": what 70 million readers' comments on the *Guardian* reveal about hostility to women and minorities online. *Feminist Media Studies* 18 (4): 592–608.

Garza, Alicia. 2014. A herstory of the #BlackLivesMatter movement. *The Feminist Wire*, 7 October. https://thefeministwire.com/2014/10/blacklivesmatter-2/ Accessed 12 April 2019.

Gay, Roxanne. 2017. Dear men: it's you, too. *New York Times*, 19 October.

Gitt, Tammie. 2018. National focus on harassment sparks local discussions. *Sentinel* (Carlisle, Pennsylvania), 3 January.

Hackworth, Lucy. 2018. Limitations of "just gender": the need for an intersectional reframing of online harassment discourse and research. In *Mediating Misogyny: Gender, Technology & Harassment*, Jacqueline Ryan Vickery and Tracy Everbach eds., 51–70. Cham: Palgrave Macmillan.

Hanisch, Carol. 2010. Women's liberation consciousness-raising: then and now. *On the Issues* Spring. https://www.ontheissuesmagazine.com/2010spring/2010spring_Hanisch.php. Accessed 2 April 2019.

Hemmings, Clare and Josephine Brain. 2003. Imagining the feminist seventies. In *The Feminist Seventies*, eds. Helen Graham, Ann Kaloski, Ali Neilson and Emma Robertson, 11–24. York: Raw Nerve Books.

Jackson, Sarah J. 2016. (Re)imagining intersectional democracy from black feminism to hashtag activism. *Women's Studies in Communication* 39 (4): 375–379.

Jackson, Sarah J. and Sonia Banaszczyk. 2016. Digital standpoints: debating gendered violence and racial exclusions in the feminist counterpublic. *Journal of Communication Inquiry* 40 (4): 391–407.

Jackson, Sarah J., Moya Bailey and Brooke Foucault Welles. 2019. Women tweet on violence: from #YesAllWomen to #MeToo. *Ada: A Journal of Gender, New Media and Technology*, 15: https://adanewmedia.org/2019/02/issue15-bailey-jackson-welles/. Accessed 12 April 2019.

Jane, Emma A. 2018. Gendered cyberhate as workplace harassment and economic vandalism. *Feminist Media Studies* 18(4): 575–591.

Jane, Emma A. 2017. *Online Misogyny: A Short (and Brutish) History*. London, Thousand Oaks & New Delhi: Sage.

Kantor, Jodi. 2017. Tarantino on Weinstein: "I knew enough to do more than I did". *New York Times*, 19 October.

Kantor, Jodi and Megan Twohey. 2017. Harvey Weinstein paid off sexual harassment accusers for decades. *New York Times*, 5 October.

Lokot, Tetyana. 2018. #IAmNotAfraidToSayIt: stories of sexual violence as everyday political speech on Facebook. *Information Communication and Society* 21(6): 802–817

Loney-Howes, Rachel. 2018. Shifting the rape script: "coming out" online as a rape victim. *Frontiers* 39 (2): 26–57.

Loza, Susana. 2015. Hashtag feminism, #SolidarityIsForWhiteWomen, and other #FemFuture. *Ada: A Journal of Gender, New Media, and Technology* 5: 1–29.

M, Kaye. 2015. On #YesAllWomen, one year later. *The Toast*, 26 May. http://the-toast.net/2015/05/26/yesallwomen-one-year-later/.   Accessed   3 April 2019.

Madden, Stephanie, Melissa Janoske, Rowena Briones Winkler and Amanda Nell Edgar (2018) Mediated misogynoir: intersecting race and gender in online harassment. In *Mediating Misogyny: Gender, Technology & Harassment* eds. Vickery, Jacqueline Ryan and Tracy Everbach, 71–90. Cham: Palgrave Macmillan.

Maitland, Eileen. 2009. *Woman to Woman: An Oral History of Rape Crisis in Scotland, 1976–1991.* Glasgow: Rape Crisis Scotland.

Mantilla, Karla. 2015. *Gendertrolling: How Misogyny Went Viral.* Santa Barbara: Praeger.

Mayer, Catherine. 2018. Diary: my sexual fantasies about equality. *New Statesman*, 25 January.

McGlynn, Clare, Erica Rackley and Ruth Houghton. 2017. Beyond revenge porn: the continuum of image-based abuse. *Feminist Legal Studies* 25 (1): 25–46.

McKay, Ronald. 2018. The screen goddess at war with feminism…or is she? *Sunday Herald*, 14 January.

McKinney, Cait. 2015. Newsletter networks in the feminist history and archives movement. *Feminist Theory* 16 (3): 309–328.

McRobbie, Angela. 2009. *The Aftermath of Feminism.* London: Sage.

Megarry, Jessica. 2014. Online incivility or sexual harassment: conceptualising women's experiences in the digital age. *Women's Studies International Forum* 47: 46–55.

Megarry, Jessica. 2018a. Under the watchful eyes of men: Theorising the implications of male surveillance practices for feminist activism on social media/*Feminist Media Studies* 18 (6): 1070–1085.

Megarry, Jessica. 2018b. *"Female Performers on a Male Stage": Can Social Media Reignite the Women's Liberation Movement.* Unpublished PhD thesis, School of Social and Political Sciences, University of Melbourne.

Mendes, Kaitlynn, Jessica Ringrose and Jessalynn Keller. 2019. *Digital Feminist Activism: Girls and Women Fight Back Against Rape Culture.* Oxford: Oxford University Press.

Merkin, Daphne. 2018. Publicly, we say #MeToo. Privately, we have misgivings. *New York Times*, 5 January.

me too (n.d.) History and Vision. *Me Too*, https://metoomvmt.org/about/#history. Accessed April 2, 2019.

Mohammed, Wunpini Fatimata. 2019. Online activism: centering marginalized voices in activist work. *Ada: A Journal of Gender, New Media & Technology* 15. https://adanewmedia.org/2019/02/issue15-mohammed/, Accessed 12 April 2019.

Morrison, Jenny. 2018. Expert defends Robert Burns after claims he glorified rape. *Daily Record*, 28 January.

Mumford, Alys. 2017. Why there aren't always two sides to every story. *Engender Blog*, 24 October. https://www.engender.org.uk/news/blog/why-there-arent-always-two-sides-to-every-story/. Accessed 20 May 2019.

National Union of Journalists. 2013. *NUJ Guidelines for Journalists Reporting on Violence Against Women*. 23 September. https://www.nuj.org.uk/documents/nuj-guidelines-on-violence-against-women/. Accessed 1 April 2019.

Olson, Candi Carter and Victoria LaPoe. 2018. Combating the digital spiral of silence: academic activists versus social media trolls. In *Mediating Misogyny: Gender, Technology & Harassment* eds. Jacqueline Ryan Vickery and Tracy Everbach, 271–291. Cham: Palgrave Macmillan.

O'Neill, Tully. 2018. "Today I speak": exploring how victim-survivors use Reddit. *International Journal for Crime, Justice and Social Democracy* 7 (1): 44–59.

Orgad, Shani and Rosalind Gill. 2019. Safety valves for mediated female rage in the #MeToo era. *Feminist Media Studies*. DOI: https://doi.org/10.1080/14680777.2019.1609198.

Powell, Anastasia. 2015. Seeking rape justice: formal and informal responses to sexual violence through technosocial counter-publics. *Theoretical Criminology* 19 (4): 571–588.

Powell, Anastasia and Nicola Henry. 2017. *Sexual Violence in a Digital Age*. London: Palgrave Macmillan.

Powell, Anastasia, Adrian J. Scott and Nicola Henry. 2018. Digital harassment and abuse: Experiences of sexuality and gender minority adults. *European Journal of Criminology*, DOI: https://doi.org/10.1177/1477370818788006.

Rentschler, Carrie A. and Samantha C. Thrift. 2015. Doing feminism in the network: networked laughter and the "binders full of women" meme. *Feminist Theory* 16 (3): 329–359.

Rivers, Nicola. 2017. *Postfeminism(s) and the Arrival of the Fourth Wave: Turning Tides*. Cham: Palgrave Macmillan.

Salter, Michael. 2013. Justice and revenge in online counter-publics: emerging responses to sexual violence in the age of social media. *Crime, Media, Justice* 9 (3): 225–242.

Savigny, Heather. 2019. The violence of impact: unpacking relations between gender, media and politics. *Political Studies Review*, 26 February. DOI: https://doi.org/10.1177/1478929918819212.

Scottish Women's Aid. 2017. *Speaking Out: Recalling Women's Aid in Scotland. 40 Years of Women's Aid in Scotland*. Edinburgh: Scottish Women's Aid.

Skalli, Loubna Hanna. 2014. Young women and social media against sexual harassment in North Africa. *The Journal of North African Studies* 19 (2): 244–258.

Serisier, Tanya. 2018. *Speaking Out: Feminism, Rape and Narrative Politics,* Cham: Palgrave Macmillan.

TimesUp! (n.d.) History. https://www.timesupnow.com/history. Accessed 20 May 2019.

Vera-Gray, Fiona. 2017. "Talk about a cunt with too much idle time": trolling feminist research. *Feminist Review*, 115: 61–78.

Vickery, Jacqueline Ryan and Tracy Everbach. eds. 2018. *Mediating Misogyny: Gender, Technology & Harassment.* Cham: Palgrave Macmillan.

Way, Katie. 2018. I went on a date with Aziz Ansari. It turned into the worst night of my life. *Babe*, 13 January. https://babe.net/2018/01/13/aziz-ansari-28355 Accessed 15 March 2019.

Weigel, Moira. 2018. The internet of women. *Logic*, Issue 4. https://logicmag.io/04-the-internet-of-women/. Accessed 15 April 2019.

Weinstein, Harvey. 2017. Statement. *New York Times*, 5 October.

Williams, Sherri. 2015. Digital defense: Black feminists resist violence with hashtag Activism. *Feminist Media Studies* 15 (2): 341–358.

Williams, Sherri. 2016, #SayHerName: using digital activism to document violence against Black women. *Feminist Media Studies* 6 (5): 922–925.

Williams, Martin. 2018. Academics divided by claim Burns was "Harvey Weinstein of his day". *The Herald* (Glasgow), 22 January.

Women's Liberation Workshop (1971/2) *An Introduction to the Women's Liberation Workshop.* (Consulted at Glasgow Women's Library.)

Xiong, Ying, Moohee Cho & Brandon Boatwright. 2019. Hashtag activism and message frames among social movement organizations: Semantic network analysis and thematic analysis of Twitter during the #MeToo movement. *Public Relations Review* 45(1): 10–23.

Zacharek, Stephanie, Eliana Dockterman and Haley Sweetland Edwards. 2017. The silence breakers. *Time*, December.

Zero Tolerance. 2018. *Handle With Care: A Guide to Responsible Reporting of Violence Against Women.* https://www.zerotolerance.org.uk/resources/Full-version-of-Handle-With-Care.pdf Accessed 21 May 2019.

CHAPTER 3

Continuum Thinking

INTRODUCTION

The previous chapter focused on the relationship between survivor speech and feminist theory and activism. It was concerned with the process of feminist theory-building, and the contradictory ways media figure in this process. It stressed the importance of a structural analysis of what women share in patriarchy, as well as the ways in which these experiences are stratified by other structural inequalities, including class and race. Of course, it is not only women who are victim/survivors of sexual violence (Chap. 5), nor is it the case that sexual assault is exclusive to heterosexual contexts (Chap. 4), although this will be my primary focus in this chapter. Measuring sexual violence incidence and prevalence is notoriously fraught but a consistent pattern emerging across time and place is that sexual violence is disproportionately experienced by women and perpetrated by men (Walby et al. 2017). Feminist analysis is first and foremost about seeing these as *gendered* patterns. As R.W. Connell argues:

> Most men do not attack or harass women; but those who do are unlikely to think themselves deviant. On the contrary they usually feel they are entirely justified, that they are exercising a right. They are authorized by an ideology of supremacy. (1995: 83)

Violence against women is entirely compatible with how masculinity, and heterosexual masculinity specifically, is personally, politically, culturally and

© The Author(s) 2019
K. Boyle, *#MeToo, Weinstein and Feminism*,
https://doi.org/10.1007/978-3-030-28243-1_3

socially enacted (Chap. 4). As Susan Brownmiller famously argued, rape is "nothing more or less than a conscious process of intimidation by which *all* men keep *all* women in a state of fear" (1975/1986: 15). Rape is both a material and a discursive practice.

This chapter is similarly concerned with what is shared, as well as what is different, in women's experiences, but focuses more specifically on *types* of male violence—*sexual* violence in particular—and how they are made sense of in different contexts. It outlines the main arguments and insights of feminist theory in relation to sexual violence and considers how #MeToo has mobilised this analysis, as well as the backlash this has generated.

This chapter uses, and develops, Liz Kelly's (1988) influential notion of the continuum of sexual violence, a concept I introduce in the next section. In a recent article (Boyle 2019), I argue that the development of feminist theory and a changing policy context necessitate a rethinking of the continuum: this is even more acute given the contemporary explosion of discourse on men's sexual violence against women with which this book is concerned. Instead of thinking of the continuum in the singular, I advocate "continuum thinking" which retains the importance of building from connections whilst understanding that the range of connections made do not always sit easily together and require different continuums (in the plural). Having set out these debates, I then discuss a widely referenced interview given by Hollywood actor Matt Damon to explore the ways in which contemporary discourse around #MeToo has both exemplified continuum thinking in practice and, simultaneously, generated a backlash against the challenges this poses. This leads me to an exploration of how the sex of sexual violence can be thought of in relation to continuums both of sex (a continuum of choice and coercion) and violence (a continuum of non-consensual experiences). The sex of sexual violence has been a much contested issue within feminist theory and activism and the Harvey Weinstein case provides a useful exemplar of what is at stake in this discussion.

From "the" Continuum to Continuum Thinking

Feminists have long argued that there are conceptual intersections between the different kinds of sexual harassment and assault which have been gathered under the umbrella of #MeToo. Liz Kelly's work on women's experiences of sexual violence is the touchstone here. In *Surviving Sexual Violence* (1988), Kelly argues that the pervasive nature of men's sexual violence means that women make sense of individual actions in relation to a continuum of related experiences across a lifetime. For Kelly, the continuum can allow us to identify a "basic common character that underlies many different events" and/or "a continuous series of elements or events that pass into one another and cannot be readily distinguished" (1988: 76). Seeing individual acts on a continuum means seeing how they work *together*—in the context of a gender-unequal society—to produce particular effects on women's lives.

This holistic understanding of women's experiences in a patriarchal culture is arguably what Alyssa Milano's #MeToo tweet called for, placing experiences of different *types* of sexual violation alongside one another ("sexual harassment and assault") as well as using the affordances of social media to place the experiences of different *women* alongside one another in order to get "a sense of the magnitude of the problem". In many ways, #MeToo has been phenomenally successful in making these connections an integral component of the wider public discourse on sexual assault. But if this demonstrates the popularity of some aspects of feminist thinking in contemporary culture, the simultaneous backlash is symptomatic of the entwining of popular feminism and popular misogyny which Banet-Weiser (2018) identifies. The element of the backlash I will focus on most in this chapter is the claim that #MeToo flattens distinctions between very different types of violence, thus disadvantaging "real" victims of sexual assault by trivialising their experiences whilst simultaneously creating an environment in which *all* men are tarred with the Harvey Weinstein brush. Although this is, in important ways, a misrepresentation of feminist thinking and activism, there are also seeds of truth in these complaints which demonstrate some of the challenges of translating complex ideas into tweets and other soundbites. In this section I want to give a flavour of some of the points of contention in feminist theory, but also the ways in which social media—and mainstream media commentary—creates a series of false equivalences antithetical to a feminist analysis.

Kelly's notion of the continuum has two key elements: it allows us to establish a common character between different experiences and to understand the continuous nature of women's experiences of sexual violation in patriarchal culture, which can make it difficult for women to articulate where individual acts against them begin and end. It is this latter point that is perhaps most challenging, particularly in a social media context. It is important to stress that Kelly is not suggesting that women cannot tell the difference between being patted on the butt by a co-worker and being raped as a child (examples I will return to in relation to Matt Damon's commentary). Rather, the continuum allows us to see how individual acts of sexual aggression are embedded within existing relationships and power structures. In this context, apparently consensual sex with a partner who has previously been abusive may be difficult for a woman to disentangle from a prior experience of being raped by this man. The rape creates the context for these later interactions; it shapes the woman's ability to give consent because she knows where refusal may lead. Listening to survivors' narratives (as Kelly does) can allow us to gain a fuller understanding of what sexual assault means in the lives of women. It is *not* to say that these events are the same, nor is it to say that they should have the same consequences for perpetrators. These are distinctions I will return to.

However, in the context of #MeToo, these two rather different understandings of the continuum are arguably blurred as the platforms on which the disclosures take place de- and re-contextualise individual experiences. On the one hand, this allows the common character of different experiences of sexual violation—and, indeed, their ubiquity—to be revealed. On the other, it removes these experiences from women's life stories and creates a continuous stream where different acts segue into one another, highlighting commonalities but also creating dissonances. Scrolling #MeToo posts it is possible to encounter a #MeToo pat on the butt story next to testimony of rape. Kelly—and Milano's—point is that these experiences *are* linked, because of the ways in which they are gendered and sexualised. Both actions are an assertion of male sexual entitlement, both are about power and depend on inequality, and both work to remind women of their subordinate status. One is part of the context in which the other is made sense of. Social media allows us to see these connections, but its continuous and de/re/contextualised flow flattens their differences.

To focus, first, on the question of connection, in her account of her Everyday Sexism campaign, Laura Bates (2014: 19) notes that she was taken back when women began sharing experiences of rape as everyday sexism. After all, rape is popularly constructed as always and only devastating and, so, rare—the very opposite of the "everyday". Except that it isn't. At a societal level, rape *is* (depressingly) routine. The threat of rape is the context in which women routinely make decisions about everyday life whether or not they have experienced rape (Vera-Gray 2016). For those who have experienced rape, the consequences of that experience can be lived everyday in more and less conscious, more and less obviously traumatic ways (Brison 2002; Gay 2018; Alcoff 2018). That for some women experiences of rape can be articulated underneath the everyday sexism banner is not, then, to deny that rape can also be experienced as a violation of the everyday in very profound and life-altering ways.

Like #MeToo, Everyday Sexism also attests to more routine experiences which *in isolation* do not, typically, produce these kinds of effects. Whilst we might accept, conceptually, that they are linked, there is a legitimate question to be asked about whether these links can work—culturally and politically—to trivialise trauma. In October 2017, as #MeToo proliferated over my social media feeds, I encountered and participated in many online discussions about the boundaries and ownership of this discourse. My hesitation in sharing #MeToo was not born from the kind of trauma and silencing discussed in Kaitlynn Mendes, Jessica Ringrose and Jessalyn Keller's (2019: 125–144) work on victim/survivors' experiences of other hashtags of disclosure. Instead, it was rooted in a hesitation to claim a space within a discourse in which I was not sure I belonged, a hesitation perhaps best encapsulated (albeit retrospectively) by the different appeals of Burke's and Milano's statements of solidarity discussed in previous chapters. Milano's statement addressed me, Burke's didn't, and there was a hesitation in contributing to a discourse which might distort or minimise the kinds of experience of child sexual abuse and rape which Burke articulated and I know some of my friends share. In this hesitation was a recognition of shared experience *and* difference, a concern with how these expressions would be understood by both victim/survivors and a wider public, and a worry that disclosure was becoming culturally mandated. However, within this hesitation was also a minimisation of sexual harassment in the face of its ubiquity, a sense that it was "not that bad" which speaks to a certain resigned acceptance of rape culture (Gay 2018). I am not claiming this as a universal experience, or even a universal feminist experience, of #MeToo, rather my point is to stress that the boundaries and purpose of #MeToo and other hashtags of disclosure have been the objects of both personal (e.g. Mendes et al. 2019: 125–144) and public (e.g. Serisier 2018: 93–116) debate from the outset.

But rape isn't just made meaningful in relation to other forms of (sexual) violence. Kelly's *Surviving Sexual Violence* (1988), alongside other important survivor-centred studies (e.g. Gavey 2005; Alcoff 2018), points to the ways women make sense of sexual violence in relation to their experiences and expectations of gender and (hetero)sexuality. This can mean understanding rape on a continuum with other *sexual* experiences: a continuum of choice and coercion in which women might understand experiences as occupying something of a "grey" area legally and/or discursively (Anitha and Gill 2009: 165; Hindes and Fileborn 2019). For instance, in their work on forced marriage, Sundari Anitha and Aisha Gill (2009: 165) refer to consent and coercion in marriage as "two ends of a continuum, between which lie degrees of socio-cultural expectation, control, persuasion, pressure, threat and force". As with the research which led Kelly to propose the continuum of sexual violence (1988), Anitha and Gill are able to highlight important connections between women's everyday experiences of constraints on marital consent and criminal, violent acts against them. Importantly, this allows them to see parallels in women's experiences across cultures (also Alcoff 2018: 152). Anitha and Gill are interested in two ways of conceptualising forced marriage, then: as part of a "continuum of choice and coercion" (2009: 165) linked to limitations imposed by culturally specific, hetero-sexualised gender roles; and as "a specific manifestation of a wider prob-lem of violence against women" (Anitha and Gill 2009: 166). They are concerned with dismantling binary ways of thinking which have disad-vantaged women (not least in the legal system) when their experiences have occupied a "grey area" in-between coercion and consent, or vio-lence and non-violence. Of course, these two conceptualisations are linked: compulsory heterosexuality is enforced by violence; violence is underpinned by constructions of heterosexually appropriate gender roles (Gavey 2005; Hindes and Fileborn 2019). But they are not the same: women can and do make positive choices about heterosexuality and mar-riage—which is not to say all women can or do.

This returns us to the tension between seeing these experiences as potentially (though not necessarily) continuous in a life story, and under-standing the importance of the differences between them in other con-texts. The context which is perhaps most relevant here is criminal justice. In a 2012 review of feminist scholarship on men's violence against women, Kelly notes an overwhelming focus on *crime* in the 15 years since her foundational text had been published. This means, she argues (2012: xix), that the "everyday, routine intimate intrusions" which had been founda-tional to her conceptualisation of the continuum had not, at that point, received sustained feminist attention (also Adur and Jha 2018). At the same time, the emphasis on crime had some side-effects antithetical to feminist concerns, including a racialised emphasis on crime control (Alcoff 2018: 225–235; Bumiller 2008) and the mobilisation of rape discourse by Western governments to justify culturally, politically and economically imperialist projects (Phipps 2014: 41). The return to the continuum—and to "grey areas"—in feminist scholarship therefore takes place in a context where crime has become a dominant framework for understanding (and responding to) sexual assault. This can sit uneasily with an approach which centres women's experiences across a lifetime, and can unsettle the very language we use to link these experiences together and so bring them into feminist consciousness and, beyond that, to the public domain.

For instance, in *Just Sex: The Cultural Scaffolding of Rape*, Nicola Gavey (2005) notes that the legalistic discourse of rape does not do justice to women's understandings of their experiences, even when their experiences might sit within a legal definition of rape. Instead, the women in her research make use of a range of different terms including forced sex, unwanted sex, coerced sex, unjust sex, obligatory sex and sort-of-rape. More recently, Linda Martín Alcoff's *Rape and Resistance* uses the term "sexual violation" which she explains as follows:

> To violate is to infringe upon someone, to transgress, and it can also mean to rupture or break. Violations can happen with stealth, with manipulation, with soft words and a gentle touch to a child, or an employee, or anyone who is significantly vulnerable to the offices of others. Sometimes the phrase "sexual violence" is used as a metaphor to stretch its meaning to encompass such events, but this is misleading. Violence is not determinative of what we are after. What we are concerned with is a violation of sexual agency, of subjectivity, of our will. We should also be concerned with the ways in which our will has been formed. (2018: 12)

A foundational element in Alcoff's thinking is her own experiences of violation. In the opening pages of her book, she describes waking, aged 16, to find a boyfriend having sex with her (2018: 6). For Alcoff, describing this incident as rape is not helpful or true to how she experienced it, but she does recognise it as violation. She later reveals earlier experiences of being raped aged nine (2018: 21–22), which she understands very differently. These differences are marked not only in the nature of the acts, but in the nature of the relationships in which they were embedded, how they were understood by the perpetrators and how they impacted on her life. This is the continuum as Kelly initially envisaged it: women making sense of experiences cumulatively, relationally and culturally.

However, this also points to one of the more challenging elements of Kelly's original conceptualisation: namely, her insistence that placing women's experiences on a continuum is *not* intended to establish a hierarchy of seriousness or injury (with the exception of sexual murder). Alcoff presents her own experiences within a hierarchy of sorts, although she is clear that these kinds of hierarchies are by no means absolute, but rather context-dependent. That Alcoff resists labelling her experience at 16 as rape does not mean that other women can or should, nor does it tell us anything about the effects of such an experience on other victim/survivors. One of the most striking things in Roxanne Gay's collection of victim/survivor writing *Not That Bad* (2018) is the cultural and social ubiquity of the hierarchy of seriousness and the damage this does to victim/survivors. Account after account demonstrates victim/survivors of any gender forced into a narrative of comparison which frustrates their attempts to seek support or justice: it wasn't that bad; at least he didn't kill me; I'm lucky because I survived. If we genuinely listen to survivors, we will always hear a *diversity* of experiences and interpretations: this, as Kelly (1988) argues, undermines the possibility of a straightforward hierarchy of seriousness or injury.

In other contexts—for instance when we think about the criminal justice system and appropriate consequences for perpetrators—hierarchies are unavoidable. But this is not the only way to think about perpetrators.

Fiona Vera-Gray's recent work on street harassment (2016) is helpful here. Like Kelly, Gavey and Alcoff, Vera-Gray is also trying to make sense of experiences of violation which are not always recognised as such by women, yet have concrete impacts on the way we live our lives. For instance, in a context where women learn to see ourselves as sexual objects, intrusions such as catcalling may at times be experienced as wanted or desired (2016: 7). Yet women make routine adjustments to our own behaviour to manage, ameliorate and, at times avoid, these kinds of behaviours. Vera-Gray also demonstrates the value of using women's experiences to understand men's behaviours, noting the sense of (sexual) entitlement underpinning men's behaviour *in contexts where consent is never sought*: "in practicing intrusion [men] are unaware of whether particular practices are wanted by individual women" (ibid). Whether an individual woman experiences a specific act of catcalling as desirable, amusing, annoying, threatening or triggering is, therefore, at least in some respects, immaterial to how the act of catcalling functions as an expression of male entitlement to, and domination over, women in public space. Catcalling is clearly in no way equivalent to the child rape Alcoff discusses, but both are linked on a continuum not only of women's experiences (where the threat or experience of one is the context in which the other is made meaningful), but also on a continuum of men's sexual entitlement and gendered power.

Indeed, Kelly always envisaged the continuum model as applicable to men's behaviour as well as female experience, to allow us to explore and expose the inter-relationships between what is constructed as "normal" and "aberrant" for men (1988: 75). I explore men's behaviour more fully in Chaps. 4 and 5, but here I want to note that this in itself demonstrates the limitations of thinking of the continuum in the singular (Boyle 2019). Thinking about men's and women's experiences can produce very different understandings of the same behaviours. Echoing Vera-Gray's work, popular discussions around #MeToo have demonstrated that sexual harassment does not need to involve physical violence or sexual assault (behaviour that is clearly marked as "aberrant") for it to have both material and psychological impacts on women. Speaking on the BBC panel show *Have I Got News For You,* comedian Jo Brand captured this point beautifully in her response to a male panellist's dismissive comment that emerging reports of sexual harassment in the Westminster Parliament were not "high level crimes":

> I know it's not high level, but it doesn't have to be high level for women to feel under siege in somewhere like the House of Commons. And actually, for women, if you're constantly being harassed, even in a small way, that builds up. And that wears you down. (BBC1 3 November 2017)

#MeToo has been highly effective in bringing to the fore these kinds of experiences and the on-going work this requires from women to continually make judgements about safety and risk in public and private interactions. In her comments, Brand reorients what, following Kate Manne (2018), we can call a himpathetic discourse which centres men's behaviour (these aren't high level crimes but normal behaviour), to insist on understanding these actions on a continuum of women's experiences across a lifetime. These experiences trouble easy categorisations: in themselves, they may not be violence (Alcoff's "violation" or Vera-Gray's "intrusion" are perhaps more accurate), but cumulatively they produce effects which limit women's capacity for action in the public, political sphere.

Part of the reason this has been troubling for contemporary commentators trying to make sense of #MeToo is that sexual violation has become so embedded in a discourse of crime—not only in scholarship, as Kelly

(2012) argues, but also in popular culture—that linking normal and aberrant behaviours in this way is too easily assumed to be re-positioning "normal" male behaviour (and, so, "normal" men) as criminal. The concern here is *what this means for men* and Harvey Weinstein is the standard against which other men are judged. Variations on the phrase "he's no Harvey Weinstein" permeate popular discussions of the reach of #MeToo as though being investigated for rape and sexual assault in multiple jurisdictions is the benchmark against which men's behaviour should be judged. This kind of commentary also depends upon an assumption that perpetrators are easily recognisable types and—as I explore in Chap. 5—Weinstein is deployed here as an aesthetic as much as a behavioural benchmark, making it easier to know where to draw the line at a glance. There is a conflation of consequences in much of this commentary where reputational damage (however temporary) is itself described in a language of violation so that men-behaving-badly are recast as the victims of indiscriminate moral righteousness.

Take, for example, David Sexton's article in *The Evening Standard* where he claims that:

> allowing no differentiation, refusing any appeal, #MeToo is developing into a general disparagement of all men—although women may deny it. (Sexton 2018)

Note that here #MeToo is positioned as the active agent, aligned with a process of justice (cast in the role of judge and jury) in which men are victims, and women are the ones offering denials, echoing Catharine MacKinnon's (2018) concerns about the roles assigned men and women in sexual harassment narratives which I cited in Chap. 1. One of the more bizarre, but telling, aspects of this article is the way it conflates men's very different experiences of being "shamed" in the #MeToo era, picturing Aziz Ansari and Matt Damon as exemplars who have been "called out online". Comedian Ansari, as discussed in the last chapter, was the focus of the "bad date" article (Way 2018) which led to a very public debate about whether his behaviour constituted violation or bad manners. Damon—who I will return to in a moment—is referenced here because of his widely criticised comments on #MeToo, not because of any accusations of abuse or sexual misconduct against him. With Ansari and Damon as the fall guys, Sexton suggests that #MeToo has created a hostile, threatening climate for *all* men. It is notable how often an amorphous #MeToo is recast in the role of perpetrator, with the victims in its sights ranging from the perpetrators themselves to anyone, male or female, who expresses any kind of reservations about "the movement". For instance, when actor Sharon Stone gave an interview in which she suggested a need for proportionality in punishments for perpetrators, the *Mail on Sunday* claimed the actor's words "put her *at risk* of a #MeToo backlash" (Zoellner 2018, emphasis added).

Some of the highest profile backlashes against #MeToo have been comments like Damon's or Stone's about the potential *consequences* of victim/survivor speech for perpetrators accused of vastly different behaviours, not all of which are recognisably criminal. This cedes a huge amount of power to victim/survivor speech and hinges on an assumption that the purpose of that speech is retribution against named perpetrators. The possibility of holding perpetrators to account is not mentioned in either Burke's Me Too origin story or in Milano's call for speaking out under the hashtag of disclosure. In both, the central concern is with how women sharing their experiences can allow for a fuller understanding of those experiences, which is also the foundation of Kelly's work. As Alcoff argues: "Accounts of responsibility should flow *from* a more fully accurate description, rather than constraining our ability to develop that description" (2018: 161).

Moreover, the claims about #MeToo's indiscriminate over-reach ignore the role of legacy media in amplifying, and often distorting, survivor-speech and activist-speech such that a public allegation is equated with a criminal, and career-destroying, sanction. To then recast the hashtag associated with victim/survivor speech as a potential threat—putting Sharon Stone *"at risk"*—brings this full circle, neutralising #MeToo by making it a source of violation. As discussed in the Introduction, it is not at all clear who or what #MeToo *is* in stories such as these, but it seems to be a stand-in for a caricature of feminist activism and theory. At the same time, insights from feminism—including the importance of continuum thinking—are often presented as common sense. Take, for instance, these two quotations from the *Los Angeles Times*:

> [...] we need to be clear about the difference between sexual assault and horny dudes who move too fast on dates. Both may exist on a continuum of disrespect for women, but one is not the same as the other. (Abcarian 2018)

> [...] we need to accept that misbehaviour is not black or white, but falls along a continuum. At one end is the rapist/sexual predator, and at the other end is the obnoxious filth. As of yet, the MeToo movement has not grappled with this reality (Davidson 2018).

Importantly, both of these articles are focused on men: the first is a response to the "bad date with Aziz Ansari" article, the second is a first-person account from a woman whose ex-partner has had #MeToo allegations made against him. These himpathetic (Manne 2018) responses encourage us to refocus women's experiences around speculations about men's motivations in order to reinforce a line between "good" and "bad" men. At the same time, these writers position that line by drawing on the continuum metaphor in order to establish a hierarchy, precisely what Kelly (1988) resisted.

Kelly's resistance to the hierarchy was not driven by a resistance to a hierarchy *of consequences*. It was a resistance to hierarchising women's experiences. Thinking about women's experiences means thinking about the ways in which our sexual subjectivity is shaped by encounters such as the one with Ansari in a broader context where we routinely make calculations about our safety in the knowledge of sexual violence, whether we have personally experienced it or not (Alcoff 2018; Vera-Gray 2016). This is *not* to assert that women experience behaviours on the continuum—from the pat on the butt to child molestation—as equivalent or identical but rather to note that meaning is not always self-evident from a simple description of the behaviour: experiences cannot be understood independent of context. In the next section, I provide a more detailed example of the ways in which continuum thinking is distorted in media debates about #MeToo.

Damonsplaining

In December 2017, actor Matt Damon gave a television interview with Peter Travers in which he was asked to comment on "the age of people charged with sexual misconduct". It is worth quoting Damon at some length as his comments bring together a number of the issues which have concerned me in this chapter so far:

> Matt Damon: I think we're in this watershed moment. I think it's great. I think it's wonderful that women are feeling empowered to tell their stories, and it's totally necessary … I do believe that there's a spectrum of behavior, right? And we're going to have to figure—you know, there's a difference between, you know, patting someone on the butt and rape or child molestation, right? Both of those behaviors need to be confronted and eradicated without question, but they shouldn't be conflated, right? You know, we see

somebody like Al Franken, right?—I personally would have preferred if they
had an Ethics Committee investigation, you know what I mean? It's like at
what point—you know, we're so energized to kind of get retribution, I
think.

And we live in this culture of outrage and injury […]... The Louis C.K.
thing, I don't know all the details. I don't do deep dives on this, but I did
see his statement, which kind of, which [was] arresting to me. When he
came out and said, "I did this. I did these things. These women are all telling the truth." And I just remember thinking, "Well, that's the sign of
somebody who—well, we can work with that" ... […]

And the fear for me is that right now, we're in this moment where […]
the clearer signal to men and to younger people is, deny it. Because if you
take responsibility for what you did, your life's going to get ruined ...

I mean, look, as I said, all of that behavior needs to be confronted, but
there is a continuum. And on this end of the continuum where you have
rape and child molestation or whatever, you know, that's prison. Right? And
that's what needs to happen. OK? And then we can talk about rehabilitation
and everything else. That's criminal behavior, and it needs to be dealt with
that way. The other stuff is just kind of shameful and gross, and I just think
... I don't know Louis C.K. I've never met him. I'm a fan of his, but I don't
imagine he's going to do those things again. You know what I mean? I
imagine the price that he's paid at this point is so beyond anything that
he—I just think that we have to kind of start delineating between what these
behaviors are.[1]

Although Damon asserts here that there is a singular spectrum or continuum—with "child molestation" at its outer reaches—he is actually
discussing two intersecting, but non-continuous, continuums: a continuum of experience (the women empowered to tell their stories); and a
continuum of sanction (paying the price doesn't have to involve prison).
More significantly, for my argument, Damon's use of the spectrum or
continuum is to insist on *distinction* as though the #MeToo version of
connection precludes this possibility. Indeed, in coverage of #MeToo
more broadly, to *compare* behaviours like the pat on the butt and child
molestation, is widely asserted to be a *conflation* of those behaviours
(e.g. Loughrey 2018).

Part of the reason Damon insists on the distinction is to enable a clear
categorisation of good and bad men. Thus, he insists that Democratic
Senator Al Franken (who resigned in the light of stories of groping and
non-consensual kissing) and comedian Louis C.K. (who admitted mastur-
bating in front of non-consenting women) are not to be understood as

belonging to the "same category" as Harvey Weinstein or Kevin Spacey. Although Spacey is not named, as the highest-profile figure accused of child molestation in this period he is an implicit presence. That the reports about Spacey focused on behaviour towards boys is also significant in allowing Damon to maintain a sense of the boundaries of heterosexual masculinity. Moreover, the very visibility of Franken and Louis C.K.'s behaviour is an alibi in itself. Later in the interview, for instance, Damon references a widely discussed photograph of Franken groping a woman, whilst Louis C.K.—who Damon says he is a fan of—made self-deprecating "jokes" about public masturbation in his successful stand-up routines. There is a tautological sense here that it couldn't have been that bad because we "all" saw it, but didn't accord it any significance (Chap. 4): because we didn't think it was bad, it can't be bad. This is also suggestive of the cultural and political value Damon accords to Franken's and Louis C.K.'s continued visibility, in comparison both with the women they groped or exposed themselves to, and also with Weinstein. One of the interesting factors about Weinstein is that whilst he was instrumental in many of the most critically celebrated films of the 1990s—including Damon's own breakthrough, *Good Will Hunting* (dir. Gus Van Sant 1997)—as a behind-the-scenes player, the films associated with him do not necessarily visibly bear his imprint. As such, their cultural standing and viewers' enjoyment of them are not imperilled by his demise. Compare this with the way in which Damon's own enjoyment of Louis C.K. as a performer is brought to bear on his judgement of his behaviour.

Damon's argument seems to be that all of these things have been conflated in the #MeToo moment: a regular, but rarely evidenced, claim against #MeToo. Damon was roundly criticised for his comments, not least for assuming interpretative authority over the meaning of women's experiences and using this to determine appropriate consequences for accused men, based on his affective affinities with them (e.g. as a fan of Louis C.K., or political ally of Franken). Among those criticising Damon on social media were Alyssa Milano (@Alyssa_Milano) and his ex-girlfriend Minnie Driver (@driverminnie). Their criticisms assert a feminist understanding of continuum thinking, noting both that women's experiences of intrusion and violation are routine, and that this means that individual acts cannot be understood in isolation as Damon's hierarchy of seriousness asserts. As Milano put it, "It's the micro that makes the macro":

We are not outraged because someone grabbed our asses in a picture. We are outraged because we were made to feel this was normal. We are outraged because we have been gaslighted. We are outraged because we were silenced for so long. (@Alyssa_Milano, 15 December 2017).

However, tracking mainstream coverage of Damon's comments and the responses to them, it is striking that it is the abstracted acts—the pat on the butt and the child molestation—which are remembered, *not* his misplaced defence of Franken and Louis C.K. This means that Damon can be (re)constructed as an imperilled speaker of truth, "under fire from feminists" (Schuster 2018) for daring to assert the self-evident differences between these acts. Notably, the ways in which the responses to Damon's comments are reported, often many months after the fact, position Damon as a victim of (feminist) violence. Perhaps the most extreme, though by no means isolated, example of this is director Terry Gilliam's widely quoted comment that Damon "came out and said that all men are not rapists, and he got *beaten to death*" (quoted in Kilkenny 2018, emphasis added). As I was finalising this chapter—more than 16 months on from Damon's interview—an interview with actor Mads Mikkelsen was published using similarly hyperbolic language: "one wrong word and you're a dead person" Mikkelsen is reported as saying, before suggesting of Damon:

He said something quite common sense and he got fucking slaughtered, so this is not a healthy discussion anymore. (Mumford 2019)

The Damon story is a cautionary one on which to end this part of my discussion of continuum thinking for a number of reasons. Firstly, and most importantly, it demonstrates the extent to which continuum thinking remains a radical feminist project precisely because it is so unsettling to binary, himpathetic ways of thinking which dominate in contemporary Western cultures. Milano's #MeToo was—and is—threatening precisely because it sought to establish connections between diverse experiences of "sexual assault and harassment", not all of which can be understood as criminal. As a result, for commentators like Damon, Gilliam and Mikkelsen, #MeToo is discursively excessive and indiscriminate. For this to make sense two simultaneous manoeuvres need to occur: women's understanding of the connections between their experiences needs to be reconstructed as an inability to distinguish between otherwise very distinct actions; and this needs to put men, all men, in jeopardy as the distinction between an alleged serial abuser like Harvey Weinstein and the rest no longer holds. This means a story of consensus-building—women *sharing* their experiences in order to build an analysis based on their common elements—can be recast as a more media-friendly story of conflict in which there are two opposing, and gendered, "sides" (Mumford 2017). That the Damon story has the additional frisson of pitting ex-lovers Damon and Driver on opposing sides makes it clear that this is in itself a sexualised story about sexual behaviour and morality, rather than violence and power.

Secondly, the Damon story exemplifies Angela McRobbie's (2009) arguments about the "double entanglement" in which feminism is taken into account in popular culture only to be disavowed. Thus, Damon (and his supporters) can be cast as the decent, upstanding inheritors of feminism and their "insights" are adopted as common sense: yes, these things are connected; no, they're not the same. At the same time, contemporary feminism—encapsulated by #MeToo—is that which threatens the legacy of feminism by exceeding common sense. In this mediated reconstruction, men doing feminism are reasonable, and yet are unfairly pilloried; whilst women doing feminism are hysterical, yet unfairly given discursive prominence—an argument which resonates with previous feminist analyses of media representations of rape (Moorti 2002: 113–148). Moreover, because this is essentially a story about speech, the response to Damon can be presented as a story about censorship: silence breaking becomes silencing.

Damonsplaining thus offers a way of talking about sexual assault and harassment through a himpathetic lens (Manne 2018) which centres questions of morality and sexual behaviour. However, in feminist hands, continuum thinking *can* be about seeing the connections between "normal" sex and sexual violence, and it is to this fraught understanding that I now turn.

Violence or Sex, Violence and Sex[2]

A view still commonly and supportively attributed to feminists in popular discourse around rape is that rape is about violence *not* sex (Bevacqua 2000: 58–60). Such binary thinking is at odds with continuum thinking, but fits more easily into mass media narratives which demand simplicity and moral clarity.

The violence-not-sex formulation seems to have its origins in Susan Brownmiller's *Against Our Will: Men, Women and Rape* (first published in

1975), or, perhaps more accurately, in the way the arguments of the book were taken up both in feminist campaigning and in popular discourse. Tellingly, in the personal statement which prefaces *Against Our Will*, Brownmiller positions herself as "a woman who changed her mind about rape" (1975/1986: 9). Brownmiller's journey, as sketched in these few pages, is from being a journalist "who viewed a rape case with suspicion", before her "moment of revelation" at a public speak out on rape (1975/1986: 7–9).

This context is important as it highlights the extent to which the violence-not-sex analysis is a *reactive* one, emerging from a mediated context in which rape is not taken seriously, and women's stories are not heard or believed (Bevacqua 2000: 58–60). It is not accidental that Brownmiller was a journalist before she became an activist: in both roles, she was involved in making meaning of rape. Similarly, Germaine Greer's recent pamphlet *On Rape*—itself an expansion of her controversial comments about #MeToo discussed in the previous chapter—makes the quotable distinction, "Rape is not a sex crime, but a hate crime" (2018: 69). However, unlike Brownmiller, Greer's intent in making this distinction seems to be to *restrict* the category of rape to what Susan Estrich (1987) influentially (and critically) called "real rape": that is violent rape, outside of the contexts of existing sexual or romantic relationships. This she distinguishes from "banal rape" (Greer 2018: 70). Whilst I do not have space to expand on Greer's at times contradictory arguments, their significance for my purposes here is their reiteration of a violence/sex binary and participation in a still fraught debate about the sex of sexual violence.

Although it has been argued feminists moved on from the violence-not-sex position fairly quickly as limitations became clear (Whisnant 2017), as the Greer example suggests, the violence-not-sex (or, relatedly, power-not-sex) position has become something of a media shorthand for feminist understandings of sexual violence, typically linked to the second wave, or more accurately to its media (mis)representatives. It is, for instance, in evidence in some responses to the sexual assault reports naming Weinstein and others (e.g. Mayer 2017; Threadgould 2017; de Leon 2018). Here, the claim this is *not* about sex is a means of insisting on the seriousness of his actions against a cultural context that had for decades condoned his abuse as *just* sex. It is also an understandable response to Weinstein's initial statement in relation to the story in which he presented himself as a man out-of-touch with changing, implicitly *sexual*, mores, attempting to reframe the story as one about morality and culture, *not* violence and the abuse of power:

> I came of age in the 60's and 70's [sic], when all the rules about behaviour and workplaces were different. That was the culture then.
>   I have since learned it's not an excuse, in the office—or out of it. To anyone. (Weinstein 2017).

My concern is that these possibilities are constructed as mutually exclusive: if it's violence or power, it can't also be sex; if it's sex it can't also be violence or power. Whilst this is a false dichotomy which continuum thinking seeks to disrupt, it is nevertheless understandable that this lingers as a means of challenging rape myths, both in frontline services and media reports sympathetic to feminist positions.

However, as Catharine MacKinnon (1981/1987) influentially argued, the violence-not-sex position downplays the interconnectedness of violence and (hetero)sex in a patriarchal context. MacKinnon argued that by seeing rape as violence-not-sex "we fail to criticize what has been made of *sex,* what has been done to us *through* sex, because we leave the line between rape and intercourse, sexual harassment and sex roles, pornography and eroticism right where it is" (1981/1987: 86–87). For MacKinnon, it is important for feminists to understand the sex of sexual violence because sexual violence is a large part of what (hetero)sex *means,* to women as well as to men, in a patriarchal context. This means understanding certain commonalities between "what has been made of" consensual heterosex and sexual violence, as well as considering the ways in which socio-cultural understandings of heterosex and gender roles more broadly provide the ground on which sexual violence occurs.

As feminist research in this area continually emphasises, there is no one way, and certainly no right way, to survive rape or sexual assault, and a universalising narrative can make it more difficult for some victim/survivors to name their own experiences and so to seek appropriate support and redress (Estrich 1987; Gavey 2005; Powell and Henry 2017; Alcoff 2018). Here it is worth returning to the Me Too and #MeToo origin stories as the range of experiences they include within their address point to different contexts for understanding rape and sexual assault. For Tarana Burke (n.d.), the experience she implicitly shares with Heaven is one of rape. Even as both Heaven and Burke herself struggle to name their experiences, in contemporary popular accounts of Me Too there is little ambivalence about the (criminal) nature of these assaults. For Alyssa Milano,

#MeToo documents the broader continuum of "sexual harassment and abuse" in women's lives. Many of the experiences documented under the hashtag #MeToo are more clearly structured by ambivalence, by the lingering doubt about the category to which experiences belong. This is at least in part because #MeToo includes experiences that are *not* typically defined as criminal acts, even if they transgress workplace codes of conduct, but it is also because they may be understood as sex, or relatedly, as flirting or unrequited passion.

The quintessential example of this is unwanted touching: the "pat on the butt" in Damon's comments, or the hand on the knee which came to dominate discussion of the downfall of British Conservative politician Sir Michael Fallon. Fallon quit his role as Defence Secretary in Theresa May's government in November 2017 after a slew of stories pointed to his unwanted touching and kissing of female journalists. Like Weinstein, part of his response to this was to suggest that he had fallen short of (new) standards of behaviour to which he wanted to aspire (Stewart and Mason 2017). What concerns me is the way that this behaviour can be understood as an ungentlemanly mistake, a breach of etiquette. Whilst Weinstein's attempt at a similar reframing largely failed because of the seriousness and multiplicity of the allegations against him, Fallon's was partially successful, not least because the acts themselves could not easily be defined as "violence" (even if they could be understood through a lens of power). As a result, Jane Merrick—one of the women who came forward about her experiences of Fallon's unwanted touching—notes that the story was instead widely reported as a trivialised, sexualised farce: "kneegate" (Merrick 2017).

Fallon's behaviour could not easily be understood as violence, but the focus on acts in isolation allowed broader questions about power to be dodged. Reflecting on the coverage of the Westminster harassment story in the British press, feminist linguist Deborah Cameron (2017) points to the recurrent use of the word "inappropriate" in these reports. This works, she argues, to obscure who is doing what to whom. Specifically, it renders men's actions as breaches of etiquette or exemplars of bad (ungentlemanly) manners, rather than as acts experienced by another (female) person. Moreover, it evacuates context as though it is the behaviour itself which is inappropriate, not the context in which it is enacted, and makes it a purely interpersonal problem. Cameron's critique finds echoes in an article by Melissa Gira Grant (2017) which addresses "sexual misconduct", another well-worn euphemism for sexual harassment. This obfuscation—also encapsulated in the Deneuve letter discussed in Chap. 2—allows women speaking out to be constructed as a threat to male *sexual* freedom.

It is not accidental that Weinstein used non-disclosure agreements so widely and so determinedly tried to quash journalistic investigations (Kantor and Twohey 2017; Farrow 2017). Arguably, the danger to Weinstein was not that the behaviour itself became public but rather that these women's *resistance* and the mode of reporting (investigation rather than entertainment) changed the context in which it could be understood: no longer evidence of bullish but successful moviemaking in a highly sexualised and glamorised context, the investigation of their grievances placed his behaviour on a continuum of sexual abuse. Likewise, it is not that Fallon tried to kiss a female journalist which is threatening, but rather that she decided to speak out about the fact, transforming an experience about which she had felt shame and guilt, into one where the shame and guilt lay not with her but with Fallon (Merrick 2017). This is the kind of transformation which leads to the accusations that #MeToo has become a "witch hunt" against men. Men are made newly vulnerable when behaviour which has historically been rewarded or joked about is denaturalised and problematised by refocusing the narrative on how these behaviours were/are experienced by women. To return to Weinstein's non-apology, men no longer know "the rules" (Weinstein 2017).

On this point, there is a certain agreement between feminists and sexual violence apologists. What Weinstein and feminist theorists arguably share is an understanding that his behaviour was *not* inappropriate according to patriarchal logic, but rather an expression of what men are promised, what they are continually told about their position in the sexual order. Of course, where Weinstein and feminist theorists differ is in what responsibility we think individual men should bear for this. That rape is a system which benefits *all* men, as Brownmiller argues, does not mean that *individual* men are not responsible for their own behaviours within the system. A himpathetic (Manne 2018) response accepts Weinstein's terms of reference and makes this a question of sexual morality *not* power or violence. A feminist response understands that sexuality, morality, power and violence are inextricably linked. This approach allows us to see the contexts in which (hetero)sex and violence are inter-related, without conflating one with the other. Thus, we don't have to replace violence-not-sex with sex-is-violence. Instead, we can understand the continuum of choice and coercion in relation to heterosexual sex and so offer a critique of heterosex in patriarchy without insisting that heterosex is always and only violence.

Conclusion

Feminist theorisations of sexual violence have been centrally about connections: connections between different acts, between victim/survivors, and among perpetrators. In this sense, the public gathering of diverse experiences under the hashtag #MeToo is clearly doing feminist work. However, the #MeToo moment also points to the dangers of media decontextualisations (or recontextualisations) of women's experiences and the flattening of differences that can occur in a disembodied Twitter feed. Whilst I have demonstrated the continuing importance of continuum thinking in this chapter, I have also highlighted the necessity of retaining distinctions and noted a worrying tendency in mainstream media commentary to suggest that this is precisely what feminists are unable to do. In this sense, media commentary on #MeToo often echoes McRobbie's (2009) double entanglement. Thus the theoretical innovations of feminism and the decades of scholarship and activism tackling men's violence and supporting women are re-presented as a kind of "common sense" which good white men have adopted, and which #MeToo has hysterically exceeded. #MeToo also reminds us what is at stake in these discussions. For victim/survivors, this is about mis/recognition of their experiences and so the ability to seek support, advocate for justice or see oneself as belonging to a collective, a movement. For (alleged) perpetrators, this is about consequences, but also about the discursive context in which their behaviour is situated: is it criminal, immoral, unprofessional and/or old-fashioned?

The next chapter takes up questions of context more centrally, situating #MeToo in relation to rape culture and the cultural and affective values which have been—and in some contexts still are—associated with men's sexual violence against women and children.

Notes

1. The interview was on *Popcorn with Peter Travers* (ABC, 12 December 2017). Video and a partial transcript of the interview can be found here: https://abcnews.go.com/Entertainment/matt-damon-opens-harvey-weinstein-sexual-harassment-confidentiality/story?id=51792548. Accessed 24 April 2019.
2. For a longer discussion of the sex of sexual violence in feminist theory, see Boyle (Forthcoming).

REFERENCES

Abcarian, Robin. 2018. She wanted to go slow; he wanted to go fast. She told the world. Is Aziz Ansari a victim or a perpetrator? *Los Angeles Times,* January 17.

Adur, Shweta M. and Shreyasi Jha. 2018. (Re)centering street harassment – an appraisal of safe cities global initiative in Delhi, India. *Journal of Gender Studies* 27 (1): 114–124.

Alcoff, Linda Martín. 2018. *Rape and Resistance: Understanding the Complexities of Sexual Violation.* Cambridge & Medford: Polity.

Anitha, Sundari and Gill, Aisha. 2009. Coercion, consent and the forced marriage debate in the UK. *Feminist Legal Studies* 17(2): 165–184.

Banet-Weiser, Sarah. 2018. *Empowered: Popular Feminism and Popular Misogyny.* Durham, NC: Duke University Press.

Bates, Laura. 2014. *Everyday Sexism.* London: Simon and Schuster.

Bevacqua, Maria. 2000. *Rape on the Public Agenda: Feminism and the Politics of Sexual Assault.* Richmond: Northeastern University Press.

Boyle, Karen. 2019. What's in a name? Theorising the inter-relationships of gender and violence. *Feminist Theory* 20 (1): 19–68.

Boyle, Karen. Forthcoming. The sex of sexual violence. In *Handbook of Gender and Violence,* ed. Laura Shepherd. Cheltenham: Edward Elgar.

Brison, Susan. 2002. *Aftermath: Violence and the Remaking of the Self.* Princeton: Princeton University Press.

Brownmiller, Susan. 1975/1986. *Against Our Will: Men, Women, and Rape.* London: Pelican Books.

Bumiller, Kristin. 2008. *In an Abusive State: How Neoliberalism Appropriated the Feminist Movement Against Sexual Violence.* Durham, NC: Duke University Press.

Burke, Tarana. n.d. The Inception. *Me Too,* https://metoomvmt.org/the-inception/. Accessed 2 April 2019.

Cameron, Deborah. 2017. Men behaving inappropriately. *Language: A Feminist Guide* (Blog). 4 November. https://debuk.wordpress.com/2017/11/04/men-behaving-inappropriately/. Accessed 20 May 2019.

Connell, R.W. 1995. *Masculinities.* Cambridge: Polity.

Davidson, Sara. 2018. My ex was just #MeTooed. He had it coming. But it's complicated. *Los Angeles Times,* 21 January.

De Leon, Aya. 2018. In defense of Aziz Ansari's mama: how toxic masculinity undermines mothers in rape culture. *Mutha Magazine,* 23 February. http://muthamagazine.com/2018/02/defense-aziz-ansaris-mama-toxic-masculinity-undermines-mothers-rape-culture/. Accessed 25 April 2019.

Estrich, Susan. 1987. *Real Rape.* Cambridge: Harvard University Press.

Farrow, Ronan. 2017. Harvey Weinstein's army of spies. *New Yorker,* 6 November.

Gavey, Nicola. 2005. *Just Sex? The Cultural Scaffolding of Rape.* London and New York: Routledge.

Gay, Roxanne. ed. 2018. *Not That Bad: Dispatches From Rape Culture*. New York: Harper Perennial.

Grant, Melissa Gira. 2017. The unsexy truth about harassment, reprinted in *Where Freedom Starts: Sex, Power, Violence, #MeToo*, A Verso Report, 145–150. New York, Verso.

Greer, Germaine. 2018. *On Rape*. London: Bloomsbury.

Hindes, Sophie and Bianca Fileborn. 2019. "Girl power gone wrong" #MeToo, Aziz Ansari, and media reporting of (grey area) sexual violence. *Feminist Media Studies*. DOI: 10.1080/14680777.2019.1606843.

Kantor, Jodi and Megan Twohey. 2017. Harvey Weinstein paid off sexual harassment accusers for decades. *New York Times*, 5 October.

Kelly, Liz. 1988. *Surviving Sexual Violence*. Cambridge: Polity.

Kelly, Liz. 2012. Standing the test of time? reflections on the concept of the continuum of sexual violence. In: *Handbook on Sexual Violence*, eds. Jennifer M. Brown and Sandra L. Walklate, xvii–xxvi. London: Routledge.

Kilkenny, Katie. 2018. Ellen Barkin tweets "Never get into an elevator alone" with Terry Gilliam. *Hollywood Reporter* March 17.

Loughrey, Clarisse. 2018. David Schwimmer says comparing Al Franken with Harvey Weinstein was "terrible and horrifying mistake"; "we should not conflate all claims into one column of bad behaviour". *Independent*, 11 April.

MacKinnon, Catharine. 1981/1987. Sex and violence: A perspective. In *Feminism Unmodified: Discourses on Life and Law*, ed. Catharine MacKinnon, 85–92. Cambridge MA: Harvard University Press.

MacKinnon, Catharine. 2018. #MeToo has done what the law could not. *New York Times*, 4 February.

Manne, Kate. 2018. *Down Girl: The Logic of Misogyny*. New York: Oxford University Press.

Mayer, Jane. 2017. Anita Hill on Weinstein, Trump, and a watershed moment for sexual harassment allegations. *New Yorker*, 1 November.

McRobbie, Angela. 2009. *The Aftermath of Feminism*. London: Sage.

Mendes, Kaitlynn, Jessica Ringrose and Jessalynn Keller. 2019. *Digital Feminist Activism: Girls and Women Fight Back Against Rape Culture*. Oxford: Oxford University Press.

Merrick, Jane. 2017. I won't keep my silence: Michael Fallon lunged at me after our lunch, *Guardian*, 4 November.

Moorti, Sujata. 2002. *Color of Rape: Gender and Race in Television's Public Spheres*. Albany: State University Press.

Mumford, Alys. 2017. Why there aren't always two sides to every story. *Engender Blog*, 24 October. https://www.engender.org.uk/news/blog/why-there-arent-always-two-sides-to-every-story/. Accessed 20 May 2019.

Mumford, Gwilym. 2019. Mads Mikkelsen: "One word wrong and you're a dead person". *Guardian*, 25 April.

Phipps, Alison. 2014. *The Politics of the Body: Gender in a Neoliberal and Neoconservative Age*. Cambridge: Polity.

Powell, Anastasia, and Nicola Henry. 2017. *Sexual Violence in a Digital Age*. London: Palgrave Macmillan.

Schuster, Dana. 2018. Oscars 2018: Will anyone talk to this man? *New York Post*, 4 March.

Serisier, Tanya. 2018. *Speaking Out: Feminism, Rape and Narrative Politics*, Cham: Palgrave Macmillan.

Sexton, David. 2018. #MenToo. *The Evening Standard*, 26 January.

Stewart, Heather and Rowena Mason. 2017. Michael Fallon quits as defence secretary saying his behaviour has "fallen short". *Guardian*, 1 November.

Threadgould, Michelle. 2017. Harvey Weinstein allegations: it's all about power, not sex. *CNN*, 6 October. https://edition.cnn.com/2017/10/06/opinions/harvey-weinstein-threadgould/index.html Accessed April 25 2019.

Vera-Gray, Fiona. 2016. *Men's Intrusion, Women's Embodiment: A Critical Analysis of Street Harassment*. London & New York: Routledge.

Walby, Sylvia, Jude Towers, Susie Balderston, Consuelo Corradi, Brian Francis, Markku Heiskanen, Karin Helweg-Larsen, Lut Mergaert, Philippa Olive, Emma Palmer, Heidi Stöckl and Sofia Strid. 2017. *The Concept and Measurement of Violence Against Women and Men*. Bristol: Policy Press.

Way, Katie. 2018. I went on a date with Aziz Ansari. It turned into the worst night of my life. *Babe*, 13 January. https://babe.net/2018/01/13/aziz-ansari-28355

Weinstein, Harvey (2017) Statement. *New York Times*, 5 October.

Whisnant, Rebecca. 2017. Feminist perspectives on rape. *The Stanford Encyclopedia of Philosophy* (Fall 2017 Edition), ed. Edward N. Zalta. https://plato.stanford.edu/archives/fall2017/entries/feminism-rape/. Accessed 1 August 2018.

Zoellner, Danielle. 2018. "You can't charge a person with murder when they've only got a parking ticket": Sharon Stone clams Harvey Weinstein – but risks #MeToo backlash as she warns against punishing all sexual predators the same way. *Mail on Sunday*, 27 January.

CHAPTER 4

The Cultural Value of Abuse

INTRODUCTION

This chapter shifts focus from acts of sexual violation, and the ways in which they are (not) understood, to consider the wider culture in which these acts became both possible and excused, if not actively enabled.

My arguments here intersect with existing feminist scholarship around rape culture (Buchwald et al. 1993). Feminists coined the term rape culture in the mid-1970s to refer to "the cultural practices that reproduce and justify the perpetration of violence" (Rentschler 2014: 67), consistent with the feminist emphasis on sexual violence as a structural rather than individual problem. Feminist work tackling rape culture has had unprecedented visibility in recent years (Phillips 2017: 2–3), thanks in no small part to digital feminist activism (Rentschler 2014; Sills et al. 2016; Mendes et al. 2019). This calling out of rape culture has encompassed on and offline protests against, for instance, the glamorisation or normalisation of rape in popular media texts, such as the Robin Thicke song "Blurred Lines" (Phillips 2017), the sexually abusive behaviour of public figures, most notoriously, Donald Trump (Maas et al. 2018) and judicial, community and media responses to rape from Steubenville (Rentschler 2014) to New Delhi (Adur and Jha 2018). As these examples suggest, rape culture encompasses both an analysis of representations which are rape supportive, *and* the ways in which actual rape and other forms of sexual violation are celebrated or trivialised culturally and socially. Thinking

© The Author(s) 2019   75
K. Boyle, *#MeToo, Weinstein and Feminism*,
https://doi.org/10.1007/978-3-030-28243-1_4

about rape culture therefore means thinking about the different inter-relationships of rape and culture, behaviour and representation, act and context.

These inter-relationships are at the centre of Roxanne Gay's post-#MeToo collection of victim/survivor testimony: *Not That Bad: Dispatches from Rape Culture* (2018). By placing victim/survivor writings in the context of rape culture, Gay and her contributors are able to retain a central focus on the difficulty of thinking about experiences of rape and other forms of sexual assault outside of the cultural context in which they occur. That context is one which creates hierarchies of victimisation—encapsulated in the book's title *Not That Bad*—which encourage victim/survivors to minimise what happened to them, whilst supporting perpetrators by disguising their abuse as something else (sex, a compliment, great art). Similarly, this chapter is concerned not only with the behaviour of bystanders or institutional practices which enable men's abuses, but also with the ways in which the stories emerging from Hollywood since October 2017 are themselves indivisible from wider discussions about the role of the media in constructing and supporting rape culture. This is not only about production contexts (though I discuss these in the next section), but also about representational practices.

Feminists have long highlighted the ways in which representation can engender harm and produce discrimination (MacKinnon 1993) and the online context has created new possibilities for representational violence which has material consequences (McGlynn et al. 2017; Powell and Henry 2017). But placing threatening language on a continuum of sexual violence should not mean equating speech—or, for that matter, memes, jokes or songs—with actual rape. This is consistent with my argument in the previous chapter about the importance of continuum thinking as a means of making connections, whilst noting the importance of clarity in relation to the *nature* of these connections and the necessity of distinction within this. As I've argued, this necessitates thinking about continuums in the plural. For instance, the abusive production practices of the media and cultural industries exposed in #MeToo testimonies are entirely appropriately positioned on a continuum of sexual violence. However, the end *products* of these industries—the song, book, theatre production, film— will not necessarily present audiences with representations of sexual violence and, even if they do, the representations will likely have a complex relationship with what happened in the production. On the other hand, products with apparently non-abusive production histories might still represent sexual violence in ways which support rape culture. To deploy another concept from Liz Kelly, the representational continuum might provide a *conducive context* (Kelly 2016) for additional, material acts of sexual violence: legitimating and supporting a culture of male sexual entitlement, dominance and coercive control (Boyle 2019). That the term rape culture can encompass these different continuums does not necessarily blunt its usefulness but it does mean that it is not always clear what we are talking about when we talk about rape culture.

Partly as a result of this confusion, in this chapter I want to refocus the discussion of context to instead think about the different cultural *values* which are accorded to abuse in the film and television industries. There are, of course, many manifestations of this, and "auteur apologism" (Marghitu 2018) is perhaps the most widely commented upon. The logic of auteur apologism is that the value of the great art produced by the abuser outweighs the importance of the abuse. This is a discourse Weinstein himself championed when he organised a petition in support of director Roman Polanski who fled the US after his conviction for statutory rape in 1977, arguing:

> Roman Polanksi is a man who cares deeply about his art and its place in the world. What happened to him on his incredible path is filled with tragedy, and most men would have collapsed. Instead, he became a great artist and continues to make great films. (Weinstein 2009)

This narrative hinges on the figure of the tortured artist, a highly gendered figure, who is able to create great art from his suffering: the suffering of those he abused eclipsed by the beauty of his art. Although Weinstein's defenders have attempted to mobilise the films with which he is associated as evidence of his continuing cultural value (Sullivan 2019), this has largely been unsuccessful. There are many reasons for this, including the scale of abuses with which he is now associated, as well as the lesser cultural value accorded to the role of the producer and distributor. This does not mean that competing notions of cultural value have not been at stake in Weinstein's decades of (alleged) abuse, as we will see. How we might now use this knowledge in shaping canons, curricula and ethical consumption is a very live question (Brooks 2017; Parkinson 2017; Silverstein 2017; Harrison 2018). The website Rotten Apples positions this knowledge in the context of ethical consumption, allowing concerned viewers to identify whether films are tainted by association with sexually abusive cast members, screenwriters, executive producers or directors and to link "to social action you can take to help restore its value".[1] Whilst this is an important effort to keep the abuses associated with film industry figures visible, this chapter is both more narrowly focused (drawing on a relatively small number of examples) and broader in reach, identifying the cultural value of gender inequality and sexual violence to the film industry as a whole.

In the first section, I draw on examples from a number of my own research projects to demonstrate some of the ways sexual abusers operate "in plain sight" in these industries. For this kind of abuse to continue relatively unchallenged requires the cultural normalisation of men's sexual violation of women and this cultural normalisation functions as an alibi for abusive men, not least by rendering so many others complicit. Indeed one way of understanding the (partial) historical visibility of sexual violation is to acknowledge the cultural value of these stories for the industry. This allows men's violence to remain hidden *as violence* despite—as we have heard so often since October 2017—a prevailing sense that this is also common knowledge.

I then turn my attention to Harvey Weinstein and this allows me to develop an argument which links Weinstein's behaviour to film industry norms. Here I argue that there is (and long has been) a cultural value to sexual violation in the film industry which is exacerbated by the complex relationships between on-screen and off-screen norms. I explore the conditions in which stories of abuse can be understood as abuse and so damaging to prominent men and those in which abuse can be folded back into existing narratives of masculine success. I draw on a number of examples here, most prominently Kevin Spacey's short film response to the reports of abuse against him. This sets up the concerns of the final chapter, where I focus more specifically, on what #MeToo has meant for men.

HIDING IN PLAIN SIGHT

It has become something of a cliché of stories about celebrity abusers to note that they hid "in plain sight", that is, that they—and those around them—publicly acknowledged aspects of their abusive behaviour, providing the conducive context in which it could flourish. Before Weinstein, the most prominent celebrity example of this in the UK was (Sir) Jimmy Savile who was posthumously revealed to have been a serial sexual predator, targeting women and children over a period of nearly 50 years. In previous work, I have explored the way in which press coverage of the abuse story unfolded in the year following Savile's death (Boyle 2018a) as well how Savile's public image was extensively reworked in and through television documentaries about the case (Boyle 2018b). In both contexts I have been centrally concerned with the conditions in which Savile's abuse was both visible and yet disguised (not visible *as abuse*), and the contexts in which it could finally be acknowledged as such. I have argued that it was sexism that allowed Savile to hide "in plain sight" in his lifetime and immediately following his death, on the basis of two central points: firstly that the cultural value of sexism meant that his criminally abusive behaviour was consistent with his public persona; and secondly, that the women who tried to report Savile during his lifetime (and even immediately after his death) simply did not matter enough for this to be a risk to the reputation of a celebrity whose cultural and monetary value for the BBC extended beyond his death.

I want to briefly unpick the point about the cultural value of sexism as this is an argument I will extend to other contexts in this chapter, building on the discussion of continuum thinking. For readers for whom Savile has only become a familiar figure through the posthumous revelations, his importance for British culture is easy to underestimate, but in his heyday he was one of the BBC's biggest stars, regularly fronting *Top of the Pops* (BBC 1964–2006) as well as hosting the long-running, prime-time family entertainment show *Jim'll Fix It* (BBC1 1975–1994). His cultural ubiquity was reinforced by his persistent presence in light entertainment genres even after his death (Boyle 2018b: 393) and through his extensive charity work. On his death, he was widely described as a "national treasure" with extensive tributes in print and on television, spanning a number of months (Boyle 2018a: 1566).

Rumours circulated about Savile's sexual preferences during his lifetime but were relatively easily absorbed within a public persona which hinged on his exceptionalism. Although he abused boys as well as girls and women, the cultural value of sexism was central to Savile's ability to remain undetected as an abuser. For instance, Savile's typical greeting to women involved kissing up their arms; he routinely groped young women on camera, and made repeated "jokes" about his preference for young women under the age of consent. Watching archival footage or reading historic interviews with Savile now, his behaviour seems so obvious (Cross 2016; Davies 2014), but part of my argument is that its very visibility is part of what made this invisible *as abuse*, not least as this implicated his audience:

the millions who tuned in every week, who read the profiles, who laughed at his jokes and saw nothing amiss. Indeed, when the reports that he was a serial sexual predator were initially acknowledged after his death, they too were folded back into a dominant narrative which positioned him as a (sexual) maverick whose performances of everyday sexism were not only accepted but integral to his "national treasure" persona (Boyle 2018a: 1568–1570).

For Savile to have continued to get away with it when many of the women and children he abused *did* attempt to speak out during his lifetime, their words, their experiences, their lives had to matter less than his. Whilst this is certainly a reflection of celebrity culture and Savile's power relative to his victims, this is not the only significant factor. Many of the women and children Savile abused were marginal figures in other ways because, for instance, of perceived behavioural problems (one of his grooming grounds was an approved school for girls), mental health issues (another was a secure hospital) and physical illness and disability (mainstream hospitals). Feminists have long argued that—whether in a police station, court or the media—women reporting sexual assault face what Jan Jordan (2004) calls the credibility conundrum: it is *their* credibility which is routinely under scrutiny. Women are more likely to be believed, and for their cases to receive sympathetic media attention, if they are: either very young or very old; if they are assaulted by a stranger; if they suffer physical injury; if they are from the dominant ethnic group in the society (and if the perpetrator is not); if they are deemed sexually "respectable" (a deeply classed and racialised notion); if they haven't been drinking or taking drugs; and if they report the crime to the police immediately (e.g. Jordan 2004; Boyle 2005; Gilchrist 2010; Sela-Shayovitz 2015; Lykke 2016). These patterns have changed little since the 1980s (Soothill and Walby 1991; Benedict 1992).

In the Savile case, the highly sexualised contexts in which Savile groomed his victims—who were typically positioned as fans, either of Savile or the pop stars on his shows—damaged *their* credibility, not his: it is not incidental that fan is a derivative of fanatic and, particularly in relation to music, has long had a clearly gendered and sexualised dimension (Cline 1992; Ehrenreich et al. 1992). Whilst the women who publicly named Weinstein as an abuser were typically in very different positions of privilege than the marginalised women and children targeted by Savile, nevertheless, their credibility was still at stake because of the sexualised nature of the industry in which they worked, or aspired to work. Yes,

Weinstein was typically in a position of professional power over the women (targeting women at the beginning of their careers), but—like Savile—he was also in a position of credibility whilst the women, not least on account of their sexualised profession, were not. To be clear, to argue that film acting is a sexualised profession for women is not to pass a value judgement on women in the industry. Rather it is to illustrate the double bind in which women working in film are caught: their success depends on their sexualisation, yet their sexualisation undermines the seriousness with which they are judged not only as artists but also (as I argue in this chapter) as victim/survivors of sexual exploitation and abuse.

In previous work, I have explored the cultural and economic value of abuse to the US audio-visual porn industry (Boyle 2011) and there are parallels here worth exploring. In this work, I argue that stories about the abuse of female performers are part of the promotional culture of contemporary porn. That performers and commentators can disclose abuse whilst they are still tied to the industry suggests that these stories do nothing to damage the profitability of porn but rather contribute to its commercial appeal. Accounts of rape and horrendous physical injuries can co-exist with claims that these women actually love and take sexual pleasure from appearing in porn. This depends upon the construction of female porn performers as a breed apart, meaning there is no necessity to approach their stories with empathy. But these stories also work because the sexual instability and duplicity of women is a recurring theme in this kind of pornography, meaning that the contradictory evidence of abuse, injury and choice can sit relatively comfortably together, without troubling the reader's pornographic investments.

Events since October 2017 have suggested that conditions for women in mainstream film may not always be a million miles away from those of women in pornography. The "in plain sight" narrative similarly suggests that sexual and sexualised abuse has not just been tolerated in the industry, but has been consistent with the stories the Hollywood film industry wants to tell about itself. The sexual abuse of female creatives is woven into its mythology in the "casting couch" of Hollywood's so-called Golden Era (Zimmer 2017; Hutchinson 2017) and the stories about gendered labour which have long linked women to decadence and sexual scandal (McKenna 2011: 5). Shelley Stamp (2004), for instance, highlights the way in which celebratory discourses around cinema in its early days coexisted with cautionary tales about the excesses and false promises of careers in the industry which were typically aimed at women. There are parallels here with my study of the paratexts of contemporary heterosexual porn where I argue that women who experience sexual abuse are frequently criticised for not properly equipping themselves with an understanding of the industry before getting involved (Boyle 2011: 596). Sexualising women's ambition, whether in porn or Hollywood, makes it extremely difficult for men's behaviour to be seen as abuse as the focus is on women's choices and morality in a context of always-sexualised labour (Hardie 2017).

Indeed, one of the notable things about Hollywood #MeToo stories is how many rely on material that has been in the public domain for some time, without damaging the careers of the men involved. For instance, when I read the stories about Dustin Hoffman's pattern of sexually harassing behaviour on set (Hunter 2017; Rossetter 2017) I was reminded not only of the stories about Savile—many of these incidents were also witnessed by others who laughed—but also of an interview with Hoffman's co-star Susan George on the re-release of *Straw Dogs* (dir. Sam Peckinpah 1971) which I had cited in my PhD. In this interview, George first described how director Sam Peckinpah coerced her into the film's infamous rape scene, and then outlined how Hoffman extended his on-screen role as "wronged husband" to his treatment of her off-screen, manipulating and emotionally abusing her (Weedle 1995: 24). George's account is clearly of a different order to those of female performers raped on porn sets and there is no suggestion from George that Hoffman's behaviour constituted sexual harassment. However, it shares with these accounts a matter-of-factness about abusive behaviour, as though it is perfectly normal for male directors and actors to behave this way. Notably, George's account is not given in an article *critiquing* the industry, but rather is part of a discussion of the film's social, cultural and aesthetic significance on its cinematic re-release. Moreover, there is a sense that this role was (and is) valuable to George herself, that Peckinpah's and Hoffman's efforts helped to produce her performance in the film, casting her in a relatively passive role whereby her performance is something that is *done to her*, rather than produced through her own labour. George's account is not unique: a biography of Meryl Streep adapted for *Vanity Fair* (Schulman 2016) tells a remarkably similar story of Streep's experience with Hoffman on *Kramer* vs. *Kramer* (dir. Robert Benton 1979). Again, this is not presented as a critique of the industry: it is a matter-of-fact account of the conditions on set which produced Streep's first Oscar-winning performance. Embedded in these accounts is the normalisation of abusive male behaviour in the service of "method" acting. As Rose McGowan puts it in typically forth-right fashion:

> I have never met a female method actor. To me, "I'm a method actor" is usually synonymous with "I'm going to be a fucking dick to everybody on set" […] I've never been on a set where that bad behaviour wasn't indulged. (2018: 100–101)

These popular accounts bear investigation not (or not only) because they necessarily reveal the unvarnished truth about production cultures, but because their circulation is suggestive of the narrative of cultural value attached to them. The abuse, particularly (though not exclusively) of actresses, is part of the promotional and critical culture around film and, until #MeToo at least, could typically be admitted without negative reper-cussions for the way the films and the men involved in them were, and arguably still are, understood. Indeed the abuse may even have contrib-uted positively to movie men's public personae or to the mythology around an individual film with stories of behavioural extremes contribut-ing to narratives of artistic exceptionalism or edgy, innovative filmmaking.

In the next section, I build on the work outlined here to demonstrate how the Weinstein abuse story hid in plain sight prior to October 2017, drawing on a range of examples which have attracted renewed scrutiny since the *New York Times* story.

Weinstein and the Cultural Value of Abuse

Like Jimmy Savile, Harvey Weinstein's abusive behaviour arguably went undetected for so long partly because it was always already an open secret. In the first days of the October 2017 story, three popular culture exam-ples were widely used to demonstrate that Weinstein's behaviour was not only *known* but that this knowledge in no way detracted from Weinstein's status within the industry. All three were intended as comedy: a joke by Seth MacFarlane at the 2013 Oscars; two mentions of Weinstein in com-edy *30 Rock* (NBC 2006–2013); and finally a barely disguised Weinstein-esque character, Harvey Weingard, in the TV series *Entourage* (HBO 2004–2011).

Given what we know about Weinstein's attempts to control and manipu-late media coverage (Farrow 2017), it may seem surprising that these jokes were in mainstream circulation. Yet, portraying Weinstein as a sexually powerful bully in many ways resonated with the persona he constructed for himself: the ruthless but successful producer in the mould of the misogynist moguls of Hollywood's still-celebrated Golden Era (Hutchinson 2017). According to Matt Damon, Weinstein was proud of being an "a**hole" (Damon quoted by Spargo 2017) and the mythology around the success of Miramax depended on this larger-than-life figure, whose abusive behaviour was chronicled as passion, dogged determination, aggression, belligerence, and even explicitly as bullying (e.g. Auletta 2002; Biskind 2004; Perren 2012). Although the sexual nature of his abusive behaviour was less explicitly chronicled, never taking no for an answer was frequently portrayed as central to Weinstein's success.

At the same time, Weinstein was widely portrayed as a champion of women in film. Part of the critical narrative around the American independent film scene with which Weinstein is associated is its contradictory gender politics (Badley et al. 2016). On one hand, independent film creates more opportunities for women in creative roles; on the other, there is an emphasis on male auteurs and male-driven content in which women largely appear as male fantasies. Sex—and the sexualisation of women in particular—was key to Miramax's distribution strategy. Miramax was known for films that seemed to promise sexual content, notably by using female nudity in marketing, yet failed to deliver (Perren 2012: 116). As Dana Stevens commented in October 2017:

> Even before he was exposed as a serial abuser and alleged rapist, Weinstein was well-known for trafficking in women. The shock is just in discovering how literal, and how violent, that traffic has been. (Stevens 2017)

Of course, the Oscars were absolutely central to the Miramax and Weinstein mythologies: films he had produced or distributed were nominated for 341 awards and won 81 (Robehmed and Berg 2017), and he had been thanked in more Oscar speeches than God, with only Steven Spielberg ratcheting up more thank yous (Ziv 2017). MacFarlane's Oscar joke is therefore particularly worthy of comment.

When MacFarlane and Emma Stone presented the nominees for the Academy Awards on 10 January 2013, McFarlane addressed the nominees in the Supporting Actress category: "Congratulations, you five ladies no longer have to pretend to be attracted to Harvey Weinstein".[2] That MacFarlane was able to make these comments publicly without apparent repercussions is itself a striking contrast to the cost to women of speaking out discussed in Chap. 2. The same was not true, for instance, for Courtney Love, who warned other women not to accept invitations to Weinstein's hotel room in a red carpet interview in 2005. Referring to this interview after the October 2017 stories broke, Love wrote on Twitter:

> Although I wasn't one of his victims, I was eternally banned by CAA for speaking out against #HarveyWeinstein (@Courtney, 14 October 2017).

There was no such backlash against MacFarlane, though when his comment resurfaced in October 2017 MacFarlane issued a statement claiming that his joke "came from a place of loathing and anger" after his friend and colleague Jessica Barth had confided in him about "her encounter with Harvey Weinstein and his attempted advances" (@SethMacFarlane, 11 October). What is it that allowed MacFarlane's joke—whatever his intent—to be absorbed into Weinstein's mythology, whilst Love's comment threatened it?

The mode of delivery is obviously significant here as the joke provides a built-in alibi; but more than that, I want to suggest that the context of MacFarlane's joke focused attention on *women's* complicity. As Hutchinson (2017) argues, you didn't have to have heard specific allegations about Weinstein for the joke to work because it refers to a much-older story about women trading sexual favours for film fame. MacFarlane's joke acknowledges Weinstein's power; but in doing so, he reinforces it, upholding Weinstein's logic in reducing the women's Oscar nominations to a question of sexual contract. Numerous accounts from women coerced and abused by Weinstein attest that he would use the success of actors like Gwyneth Paltrow or Renée Zellweger as evidence of what he could do for women's careers if they acquiesced to his sexual demands. This is not to say that Paltrow or Zellweger *did* acquiesce to his sexual demands, but rather that Weinstein could credibly claim that they did precisely because of the gendered power differentials and sexualisation of women's labour in the film industry. What "everyone knew" was not just that Weinstein was abusive, but that his abuse worked:

> "Everyone knew if you were in a Harvey movie, chances are you were going to win or be nominated for an Oscar," said Sasha Stone, founder and publisher of AwardsDaily.com, an industry awards tracker since 1999. "It's a sick thing to be in a business where that was the collateral used to coerce women." (Robehmed and Berg 2017)

Even after the *New York Times* story, the success of actresses in Weinstein's movies was widely used against them, their acceptance-speech thanks used as evidence of their complicity. *Bustle* even ran a story detailing which women had, and which had not, thanked Weinstein in their Oscar speeches (Florio 2017).

There is a similar logic at play in the *30 Rock* Weinstein-moments where a female character says she successfully resisted Weinstein's advances three times (out of five) and later jokes about Weinstein passing out on top of her (Stolworthy 2017). The female character, and not the absent Weinstein, is the one sexualised through the reporting of these encounters: neither Weinstein's "persistence", nor the grotesque image conjured of the over-weight, inebriated Weinstein is at odds with his public persona. Indeed, that a man so physically unattractive by Hollywood standards could command the apparently endless attention of beautiful movie stars reinforced his success rather than detracted from it, whilst rendering the women complicit at best, sexually duplicitous at worst.

This scrutiny of women's behaviour is something I have already observed in my discussion of the discursive construction of feminism in popular discourse around the Weinstein case in Chap. 2. The promotional cultures of the film industry add another layer to this analysis as many of the women who have publicly accused Weinstein of abuse were also pictured with him at glamorous public events afterwards. The gendered nature of red carpet reporting, with the emphasis on women's clothing rather than their achievements, has long been criticised. But whilst #AskHerMore might be attempting to shift the red carpet narrative to emphasise women's achievements,[3] the conventions of these events remain skewed towards the sexualised display of women. Red carpet photographs function as something of a scarlet letter for Weinstein's accusers, sticky with shame not for Weinstein (who wouldn't want their photo taken with a beautiful woman?) but for the women. The polished, glamorous images undercut their narratives of victimisation. That they don't look or act like "real" victims has been the focus of recurring online commentary, including in numerous memes which place quotes from women's testimony over smiling red carpet photographs of them with Weinstein. There is something at stake in the fascination with the (apparent) juxtaposition of female glamour and male monstrosity. Weinstein does not embody the aesthetic norms of the industry and memes abound in which he is portrayed as the grotesque, slimy, slobbering *Star Wars'* villain Jabba the Hutt, among other characters. Although these representations are clearly not flattering to Weinstein, his monstrosity is often constructed as *their* shame as the women pose with arms around him, a signal of their apparent willingness to sacrifice their sexual morality to get ahead in the industry.

Whilst MacFarlane's comment was widely and sometimes appreciatively reported in 2017, in 2013 it was easily folded back into pre-existing narrative about women's sexualised labour in Hollywood. As Oscar host in February 2013, McFarlane's performance drew heavily on this narrative for humour, most notoriously in a comedic song "We Saw Your Boobs" in which he detailed the films in which "we" had seen the breasts of the female nominees and other women in the audience, including in films produced by Weinstein. The song included at least two examples where the actor's nudity was in a sexual assault scene—Jodie Foster *The Accused* (dir. Jonathan Kaplan 1988) and Hilary Swank in *Boys Don't Cry* (dir. Kimberly Peirce 1999)—as well as reference to the non-consensual circulation of nude images of Scarlett Johansson stolen from her phone. Moreover, the skit depended upon the reactions of some of the named women. Although these were pre-filmed, presumably with the actors' foreknowledge and consent, that they were required to play along with being the butt of a sexualised joke at an event supposedly celebrating their professional achievements is in itself a form of sexualised harassment for which MacFarlane was criticised at the time. Yet, the relatively scant reference to the skit in the extensive 2017 coverage of MacFarlane's comments about Weinstein is striking: I found only two articles (both by women) which mentioned MacFarlane's sexist performance as Oscars host alongside his alleged "outing" of Weinstein (Hutchinson 2017; Garavelli 2017).[4] MacFarlane could, as Dani Garavelli (2017) notes, "recast himself as a feminist champion using humour to expose the film industry's sexist ways" despite his own complicity in trivialising sexual abuse in that same Oscar season.

The MacFarlane example is a useful reminder that calling out individuals without examining the structural factors which enabled their abuse can only get us so far. Sexism remains so unremarkable in many ways, so embedded in cultural norms and practices that it continues to accrue cultural value even as individual monsters fall.

However, sexualised misogyny is only part of the story: the comingling of abuse, power and masculinity is a heady mix and does not, always, necessitate a female victim. In the next section, I turn my attention to Kevin Spacey who was accused of sexual assault by actor Anthony Rapp in October 2017. MacFarlane features in Spacey's story too. A 2005 scene in his animated comedy *Family Guy* shows baby Stewie running naked through a shopping mall screaming "Help! I've escaped from Kevin Spacey's basement". (Rapp was 14 at the time he was assaulted by Spacey.) When Rapp went public, Spacey's now infamous response was to try to reorient the news agenda by combining his apology to Rapp with a statement in which he came out as a gay man. Spacey was widely criticised for this, not least for his statement that enabled a slew of homophobic online commentary. However, here I want to focus not on Spacey's non-apology, but rather on a later attempt to incorporate the sexual assault reports into his star image in an astonishing short film, *Let Me Be Frank*, which he released via social media on Christmas Eve 2018.[5] In my analysis of the film, I argue that Spacey seeks to capitalise on the moral duplicity of his most celebrated character to advance his own "plain sight" argument, rendering viewers complicit. This opens up a discussion of what it means to position viewers in this way.

"You Loved It"

Let Me Be Frank is a three-minute film in which Spacey reprises his celebrated role as Frank Underwood from *House of Cards* (Netflix, 2013–2018), a role he lost in the aftermath of Anthony Rapp's public statement accusing him of sexual assault. Spacey uses the short film—released to social media following the critically lukewarm reception of Netflix's Spacey-free final season of *House of Cards*—to obliquely address the sexual assault reports and highlight the cultural costs of these allegations *for viewers*. Spacey/ Underwood reminds viewers of the pleasure they derived from his character's moral duplicity, using the direct-to-camera address frequently deployed to reveal his character's cunning and crimes in the series, making viewers complicit in their enjoyment of his nefarious schemes. The *mise-en-scène* evokes the dark, expensive domestic interiors of *House of Cards'* early seasons but, with Spacey/Underwood wearing a Santa Claus kitchen apron whilst undertaking mundane domestic chores, it also offers an ironic commentary on Spacey/ Underwood's removal from the *House of Cards'* finale. For fans of the series, the Spacey/ Underwood of *Let Me Be Frank* is thus both thrillingly familiar and uncomfortably different.

The Spacey/Underwood of *Let Me Be Frank* echoes Weinstein's non-apology in response to the *New York Times* article (Weinstein 2017), suggesting that he is being unfairly held to account for behaviour which had previously been culturally legitimated, or even celebrated. However, for my purposes here, it is Spacey's gamble that the reports of sexual assault can themselves be integrated into his star persona that is interesting. Although this was by no means uniformly successful and *Let Me Be Frank* attracted considerable mainstream media criticism (Kornhaber 2018; Segalov 2018; Zhong 2018), even a quick glance at comments on Spacey's Twitter feed or below the YouTube video demonstrate a continued investment in Spacey as an actor and Underwood as a character. Whilst, for some, this continuing investment is based on disbelieving Rapp and the other men who have disclosed sexual abuse at Spacey's hands, the victim/survivors don't have to be disbelieved for them to be disregarded. This depends on two—related, though potentially contradictory—moves: one in which the viewers' pleasure and Spacey's talent is valued above the rights of his accusers (a version of auteur apologism: he's a great actor so it shouldn't matter); the other in which the assault reports are not incoherent with their pleasure but potentially contribute to it (we've known this about Spacey all along, it's what makes him a great actor and his characters enjoyable antiheroes).

The pervasiveness of this attitude was brought home to me in an academic context, shortly before #MeToo, when two former male colleagues concluded a presentation about securing academic grants with a slide showing Kevin Spacey as Underwood with the caption "don't take no for an answer". My colleagues—however ironically they intended it—positioned themselves within Underwood's homosocial address and recognised the cultural (and potential economic) value of a particular kind of masculine performance. When I tried to challenge them on this, it was swiftly dismissed as evidence of a (feminist) lack of humour: they were telling it like it is, and I was taking things too seriously.

This refusal to hear "no" has itself become mythologised in many competitive contexts: academia, business, sport, film. Indeed, it was explicitly referenced by Uma Thurman when she told *New York Times* about her experiences on the set of *Kill Bill* (dir. Quentin Tarantino 2003, 2004) during which she sustained serious physical injury as a result of director Quentin Tarantino's approach to filming (O'Dowd 2018). Tarantino, Thurman told Maureen O'Dowd, "didn't like to hear no".

Spacey's performance in *Let Me Be Frank* is of a piece with this, promising revelation and recasting reports of abuse in relation to morality in a context where immorality is associated with the positive values of risk-taking and fearlessness. It is not supposed to be comfortable: "I told you my deepest darkest secrets. I showed you exactly what people are capable of. I shocked you with my honesty, but mostly, I challenged you and made you think," Spacey/Underwood tells us. He continues:

> We weren't afraid, not of what we said and not of what we did, and we're still not afraid. Because I can promise you this: if I didn't pay the price for the things we both know I did do, I'm certainly not going to pay the price for the things I didn't do. Of course, they are going to say I'm being disrespectful and not playing by the rules, as though I ever played by anyone's rules before. I never did, and you loved it.

Because "we" have always known what Spacey/Underwood is—like Weinstein it's not something he has hidden—it is "our" current condemnation of him which is marked as inauthentic and misjudged. We have changed the rules. He has remained consistent.

Underwood is not the only morally compromised or duplicitous Spacey character to have featured in popular responses to the disclosures of sexual abuse. As Maja Brandt Andreasen's on-going work on Spacey memes demonstrates,[6] images and famous lines of other Spacey antiheroes—including criminal mastermind Verbal Kint/Keyser Soze (*Usual Suspects*, dir. Bryan Singer 1995), serial-killer John Doe (*Se7en*, dir. David Fincher 1995) and paedophilic Lester Burnham (*American Beauty*, dir. Sam Mendes 1999)— also circulated widely in the aftermath of Rapp's statement, suggesting a continued investment in Spacey's most celebrated roles. Where Spacey emerges as the butt of the joke, it is more typically in relation to his coming out as gay. There are two main strands to this: firstly, that his coming out—like the abuse story—is not newsworthy as it, too, was already widely known; secondly, that his homosexuality becomes the butt of homophobic humour linking gay men and paedophilia. There is also a significant emphasis on what *fans* stand to lose as a result of the momentum against Spacey, something the *Let Me Be Frank* video seems to directly address.

Some of these memes suggest that the pleasure associated with Spacey's star text is not undermined by the sexual assault reports but may even be *enhanced* by it. This is most obvious when the memes address an already-knowing audience, creating a certain sub-cultural value in having always-already-known about Spacey/Underwood/Soze/Doe in which it is naïve victim/survivors and gullible media commentators who are the butt of the joke. Indeed, following the Rapp story, it was suggested that Spacey had alluded to—and sought to excuse—his misdeeds in his acceptance speech at the 2000 Oscars, when he won Best Actor for his role as Lester Burnham:

> To my friends, for pointing out my worst qualities. I know you do it because you love me, and that's why I love playing Lester, because we got to see all of his worst qualities and we still grew to love him.
> This movie to me is about how any single act by any single person put out of context, is damnable. But the joy of this movie is that it is real beauty [...]. (Spacey, quoted in Vincent 2017)

For my purposes, whether this was an admission from Spacey is not the central issue. Rather, I am interested in the way Spacey collapses the distance between himself, his character and his audience, rendering all potentially complicit, anticipating his performance in *Let Me Be Frank*. The function of this speech re-emerging in November 2017 also interests me: on one hand, this is obviously consistent with the "plain sight" narrative that I have discussed in this chapter, but in its scrutiny of Spacey's past roles and statements, this story also performs a certain kind of fan-like labour which reinstates the value of the work as a source of truth. The truth was there all along if only we'd paid attention. Spacey told us who he was, and we applauded. There are parallels here with Louis C.K. whose comedy frequently referred to public masturbation, the very behaviour he admitted to in response to a November 2017 *New York Times* exposé (Ryzik et al. 2017). C.K., like Spacey, was celebrated for, and profited from, the behaviour for which he was later condemned.

From a feminist point of view, these narratives are, therefore, contradictory, offering both a critique of rape culture and a sense that this critique carries a sense of loss (for viewers) that is a form of injustice (if "we" all knew this all along, then why should Spacey/his fans be punished for this now?). Although it remains to be seen whether Spacey will be able to return to an acting career, the sense that #MeToo has victimised fans is one which Andreasen finds in memes relating to Louis C.K. as well as Spacey. This is consistent with a wider discourse in which #MeToo is positioned as pleasure-destroying, posing a challenge not only to specific perpetrators but also to those who have invested in their careers and the cultural products with which they are associated.

Reports of Louis C.K.'s comeback appearances suggest that he is now mining this aggrieved masculinity for his comic material, although by no means to universal acclaim (North 2019). At the same time, on my commute to work I still pass billboards showing Johnny Depp advertising Dior's Sauvage (tagline "wild at heart"), three years after Amber Heard reported him for domestic abuse (which, I am bound to point out, he denies). Depp's recent *GQ* front cover (Heaf 2018) also plays explicitly on his bad boy image. He is described as an "outlaw" and the headline promises: "The divorce. The violence. The excess. The vengeance." This is a description which (minus the divorce) could map relatively easily onto many of his most successful characters. His reported abuse of Heard thus fits relatively comfortably within a supremely marketable, if somewhat maverick, version of film star masculinity. This is not to say that more critical profiles of Depp have not also emerged (Roddick 2018), but rather to argue that there are models of violent masculinity which remain culturally valued and which Dior/*GQ*/Depp are all able to draw on in contemporary representations of the actor.

There are also numerous media commentaries about whether "we" can still enjoy Woody Allen films following his daughter Dylan Farrow's reports that he raped her as a child (which, I am bound to point out, he denies). Notably, Farrow herself addressed the continued investment in her father's work directly in her 2014 open letter in the *New York Times*, which begins and ends with the question: "What's your favourite Woody Allen movie?" (Farrow 2014). In her analysis of the journalistic commentary and investigations which followed from Farrow's account, Tanya Serisier (2018) provides a compelling argument about the ways in which, prior to #MeToo, Farrow was constructed as an unreliable narrator of her own life through her failures—as well as those of her mother, Mia Farrow—to tell her story dispassionately, using legalistic frameworks, language and evidence. As a lone voice, Farrow's story lacked what Serisier (2018: 108) calls "semantic thickness", where narratives with common elements can act as cultural corroboration of each other.

However, another part of the reason Farrow's 2014 story failed to gather traction is perhaps that it posed too direct a challenge to readers, demanding an ethical action from those who work in, profit from or even watch her father's films. Farrow could therefore be cast not only as hysterical and unreliable (as Serisier argues) but also as censorious and moralising, placing "our" pleasures under scrutiny. Farrow occupies the position of the feminist killjoy par excellence (Ahmed 2010).

What Spacey's *Let Me Be Frank*, Louis C.K.'s comeback, Depp's Dior ad and Farrow's letter all have in common, therefore, is a recognition that to understand these men as abusers is to make an ethical demand on spectators which is at odds with the pleasures promised (and, for many, delivered) by their professional roles. This is not just a demand to give something up (as Farrow asks), but rather to re-examine the cultural values we have long accorded to abuse and abusers. Whilst this may lead to the "othering" of abusers in ways I explore in the next chapter, our affective investments in these men and their work makes this a more complicated process.

Conclusion

In drawing this chapter to a conclusion, I want to return to a discussion I took part in back in 2002 which predicted the cultural struggles over reports of abuse against well-known men in the #MeToo moment. I was on a panel discussing screen representations of child sexual abuse organised by the Women's Support Project in Glasgow. Also on the panel was John Yorke, then an Executive Producer on BBC1's soap opera *EastEnders*. We were responding to an episode of *EastEnders* in which Kat Slater reveals that she had been raped by her uncle as a child. In the discussion, Yorke divulged that when they were developing the child sexual abuse story, they had initially intended that it would focus on another character (Janine Butcher) being abused by her step-father (Roy Evans). Unlike Kat's Uncle Harry, who was only in the soap for the duration of this storyline, Roy was a regular and popular character. The team decided that this would alienate their viewers, who, having emotionally invested in Roy over years, would feel betrayed by such a revelation.

The #MeToo stories involving public figures parallel the one *EastEnders* felt unable to tell all those years ago. These stories involve men we think we know, doing things which prompt us to re-examine our affective investments in them. Of course, this process also takes place in families and communities in relation to non-celebrity abusers, but what has concerned me in this chapter are the wider reverberations for our understandings of film and television cultures. It is in this context that Commander Peter Spindler of the Metropolitan Police could claim that Jimmy Savile "groomed the nation" (Laville et al. 2013), and Sylvia Nicol, who worked at Stoke Mandeville Hospital (one of the charitable causes with which Savile was most aligned), could tell documentary filmmaker Louis Theroux that she is "a victim of losing those memories" associated with Savile.[7]

Whilst I am wary of using sexual assault as a metaphor in a discussion where it is also a material reality (Boyle 2018b), Spindler and Nicol do point to the way in which these celebrity stories reverberate culturally. The #MeToo moment has presented a sustained challenge to rape culture, partly by revealing how pervasive its operations have been. But this also means that it has implicated an increasing number of us: as viewers, readers, fans, subscribers, consumers, as well as victim/survivors or perpetrators. Given this is an industry we turn to for entertainment, Sara Ahmed's (2010) figure of the feminist killjoy has perhaps never been more apt. As Ahmed argues, being disappointed in something that is supposed to make us happy—that perhaps *used to* make us happy—is not only to experience negative affect but also to place us at odds with powerful cultural norms: to fail to "get" the joke, appreciate the art, enjoy the film, remember fondly. It is easier not to know. Or not to say that/what we know. At the height of #MeToo and its mainstream media coverage, I had countless conversations where friends would share their concerns about which male celebrity would be next to be accused. Running through many of these discussions was a thinly veiled concern that hearing these testimonies would—like Dylan Farrow's open letter—make concrete demands on us as ethical viewers or consumers. They would demand we gave something (pleasurable) up.

#MeToo has put the conditions of our pleasures under the microscope. Yet, as the Johnny Depp example suggests, some of the figures accused of violence have been easier to give up than others and cultural investments in violent, risky, dangerous masculinity have continued to co-exist with #MeToo. Indeed, as I write, Quentin Tarantino's *Once Upon a Time in Hollywood* (dir. Quentin Tarantino 2019) has just had its Cannes premiere to rave reviews whilst, at a press conference, the director both refused to answer the question of *New York Times* journalist Farah Nayeri about the marginal role given to women in his film, and discussed his appreciation of Roman Polanski's work (Setoodeh 2019). Whilst Tarantino has been called out on both counts by a number of commentators, even a cursory glance at Twitter responses to the press conference demonstrate an enduring investment in the notion of the male auteur and the re-silencing of women who have spoken out both during and before the #MeToo era. Thus, Tarantino can appreciate Polanki's art without reference to his statutory rape conviction, and fans can argue that Tarantino's own films have consistently privileged female actors, citing *Kill Bill*—the films on which Thurman was injured as a result of his aggressive practices—as evidence that the female journalist's question was misguided. Thurman's performance eclipses Thurman's experience and, in shoring up the male auteur, allows him to evade responsibility. All of this in the context of the release of a film set against the backdrop of the murder of Polanski's wife, Sharon Tate.

In the next chapter, I take this analysis further, exploring the conditions of male believability, firstly in relation to male victims of sexual abuse, and secondly in relation to representations of male perpetrators as more or less credible. Here I draw on two apparently contradictory feminist frameworks—Kate Manne's (2018) notion of himpathy, and feminist analysis of the male perpetrator of sexual abuse as "other" (Cameron and Frazer 1987; Kelly 1996; Kitzinger 1999)—to explore what is at stake in the representation of the celebrity perpetrator of the #MeToo era.

NOTES

1. Rotten Apples: https://therottenappl.es/ Accessed 9 May 2019.
2. The 2013 Oscar nominations can be viewed on You Tube: https://www.youtube.com/watch?v=SzNoT3Zcw2A&feature=youtu.be&t=3m9s Accessed 6 May 2019.
3. See http://therepresentationproject.org/the-movement/askhermore/
4. This is based on a Nexis search for Harvey Weinstein and Seth MacFarlane, focusing on October 2017, which returned 166 results (excluding duplicates).
5. *Let Me Be Frank*, https://www.youtube.com/watch?v=JZveA-NAIDI Accessed 30 April 2019.
6. Maja Brandt Andreasen is a PhD student at the University of Strathclyde. At the time of writing, this work is unpublished.
7. *Louis Theroux: Savile*, BBC2, 2 October 2016.

REFERENCES

Adur, Shweta M. and Shreyasi Jha. 2018. (Re)centering street harassment – an appraisal of safe cities global initiative in Delhi, India. *Journal of Gender Studies* 27 (1): 114–124.

Ahmed, Sara. 2010. Feminist killjoys (and other willful subjects). *Scholar and Feminist Online* 8 (3). http://sfonline.barnard.edu/polyphonic/ahmed_01.htm#text1. Accessed 20 May 2019.

Auletta, Ken. 2002. Beauty and the beast. *New Yorker*, 8 December.

Badley, Linda, Claire Perkins and Michele Schreiber. 2016. Introduction. *Indie Reframed: Women's Filmmaking and Contemporary American Independent Cinema*, eds. Linda Badley, Claire Perkins and Michele Schreiber, 1–14. Edinburgh: Edinburgh University Press.

Benedict, Helen. 1992. *Virgin or Vamp: How the Press Covers Sex Crimes*. Oxford: Oxford University Press.

Biskind, Peter. 2004. *Down and Dirty Pictures: Miramax, Sundance, and the Rise of Independent Film*. New York: Simon & Schuster.

Boyle, Karen. 2005. *Media and Violence: Gendering the Debates*. London: Sage.

Boyle, Karen. 2011. Producing abuse: Selling the harms of pornography. *Women's Studies International Forum* 34 (6): 593–602.

Boyle, Karen. 2018a. Hiding in plain sight: gender, sexism and press coverage of the Jimmy Savile case. *Journalism Studies* 19 (11): 1562–1578.

Boyle, Karen. 2018b. Television and/as testimony in the Jimmy Savile case. *Critical Studies in Television* 13 (4): 387–404.

Boyle, Karen. 2019. What's in a name? Theorising the inter-relationships of gender and violence. *Feminist Theory* 20 (1): 19–36.

Brooks, Xan. 2017. Reel dilemma: Are we condoning the conduct of Hollywood's tyrants by watching their films? *Guardian*, 10 November.

Buchwald, Emilie, Pamela R. Fletcher and Martha Roth, eds. 1993. *Transforming a Rape Culture*, Minneapolis: Milkweed.

Cameron, Deborah and Elizabeth Frazer. 1987. *The Lust to Kill: A Feminist Investigation of Sexual Murder*. Cambridge: Polity.

Cline, Cheryl. 1992. Essays from *Bitch: The Women's Rock Magazine with Bite*. In *The Adoring Audience: Fan Culture and Popular Media*, ed. Lisa A. Lewis, 69–83. London: Routledge.

Cross, Simon. 2016. Disclosure and enclosure: revisiting media profiles of Jimmy Savile. In *Profile Pieces: Journalism and the "Human Interest" Bias*, eds. Sue Joseph and Richard Lance Keeble, 100–115. London: Routledge.

Davies, Dan. 2014. *In Plain Sight: The Life and Lies of Jimmy Savile*. London: Quercus.

Ehrenreich, Barbara, Elizabeth Hess and Gloria Jacobs. 1992. Beatlemania: girls just want to have fun. In *The Adoring Audience: Fan Culture and Popular Media*, ed. Lisa A. Lewis, 84–106. London: Routledge.

Farrow, Dylan. 2014. An open letter from Dylan Farrow. *New York Times Blog*, https://kristof.blogs.nytimes.com/2014/02/01/an-open-letter-from-dylan-farrow/. Accessed 14 May 2019.

Farrow, Ronan. 2017. Harvey Weinstein's army of spies. *New Yorker*, 6 November.

Florio, Angelica. 2017. Here's every woman who did and didn't thank Harvey Weinstein at the Oscars. *Bustle*, 3 November https://www.bustle.com/p/heres-every-woman-who-did-didnt-thank-harvey-weinstein-at-the-oscars-2953763. Accessed 14 May 2019.

Garavelli, Dani. 2017. Faux outrage adds to agony of Weinstein revelations. *Scotsman*, 14 October.

Gay, Roxanne. ed. 2018. *Not That Bad: Dispatches From Rape Culture*. New York: Harper Perennial.

Gilchrist, Kristen. 2010. "Newsworthy" victims? *Feminist Media Studies* 10 (4): 373–390.

Hardie, Kate. 2017. Time to make the link between abuse and film content. *Guardian*, 15 October.

Harrison, Rebecca. 2018. Fuck the canon (or, how do you solve a problem like Von Trier): teaching, screening and writing about cinema in the age of #MeToo. *Mai: Feminism and Visual Culture* 9 November. https://maifeminism.com/fuck-the-canon-or-how-do-you-solvea-problem-like-von-trier-teaching-screening-and-writing-about-cinema-in-the-age-of-metoo/. Accessed 25 April 2018.

Heaf, Jonathan. 2018. Johnny Depp will not be buried. *GQ* (UK). 2 October.

Hunter, Anna Graham. 2017. Dustin Hoffman sexually harassed me when I was 17. *Hollywood Reporter,* 1 November.

Hutchinson, Pamela. 2017. Moguls and starlets: 100 years of Hollywood's corrosive, systemic sexism. *Guardian*, 19 October.

Jordan, Jan. 2004. *The Word of a Woman? Police, Rape and Belief.* Hampshire: Palgrave Macmillan.

Kelly, Liz. 1996. Weasel words: paedophiles and the cycle of abuse. *Trouble and Strife* 33: 44–49.

Kelly, Liz. 2016. The conducive context of violence against women and girls. *Discover Society*, 1 March. https://discoversociety.org/2016/03/01/theorising-violence-against-women-and-girls/. Accessed 20 May 2019.

Kitzinger, Jenny. 1999. The ultimate neighbour from hell?: stranger danger and the media representation of "paedophilia". In *Social Policy, the Media and Misrepresentation*, ed. Bob Franklin, 207–221. London: Routledge.

Kornhaber, Spencer. 2018. The disturbing truth about Kevin Spacey's "Let Me Be Frank" video. *The Atlantic*. 27 December.

Laville, Sandra, Esther Addley and Josh Halliday. 2013. Police errors left Jimmy Savile free to "groom the nation". *Guardian*, 11 January.

Lykke, Lucia C. 2016. Visibility and denial: accounts of sexual violence in race- and gender-specific magazines. *Feminist Media Studies* 16 (2): 239–260.

Maas, Megan K., Heather L. McCauley, Amy E. Bonomi and S. Gisela Leija. 2018. "I was grabbed by my pussy and its #NotOkay": A twitter backlash against Donald Trump's degrading commentary. *Violence Against Women* 24 (14): 1739–1750.

MacKinnon, Catharine. 1993. *Only Words*. Cambridge, MA: Harvard University Press.

Manne, Kate. 2018. *Down Girl: The Logic of Misogyny*. New York: Oxford University Press.

Marghitu, Stefania. 2018. "It's just art": auteur apologism in the post-Weinstein era. *Feminist Media Studies* 18 (3): 491–494.

McGlynn, Clare, Erica Rackley and Ruth Houghton. 2017. Beyond revenge porn: the continuum of image-based abuse. *Feminist Legal Studies* 25 (1): 25–46.

McGowan, Rose. 2018. *Brave.* London: HQ.

McKenna, Denise. 2011. The photoplay or the pickaxe extras, gender, and labour in early Hollywood. *Film History: An International Journal* 23 (1): 5–19.

Mendes, Kaitlynn, Jessica Ringrose and Jessalynn Keller. 2019. *Digital Feminist Activism: Girls and Women Fight Back Against Rape Culture.* Oxford: Oxford University Press.

North, Anna. 2019. Louis C.K. and Aziz Ansari have an opportunity for redemption. They're squandering it. *Vox*, 9 January. https://www.vox.com/2019/1/9/18172273/louis-ck-comeback-parkland-aziz-ansari-metoo. Accessed 20 May 2019.

O'Dowd, Maureen. 2018. This is why Uma Thurman is angry. *New York Times*, 3 February.

Parkinson, Hannah J. 2017. Kevin Spacey deserves to be scorned. But can I still watch *House of Cards? Guardian*, 2 November.

Perren, Alisa. 2012. *Indie, Inc: Miramax and the Transformation of Hollywood in the 1990s.* Austin: University of Texas Press.

Phillips, Nickie D. 2017. *Beyond Blurred Lines: Rape Culture in Popular Media.* Lanham: Rowman and Littlefield.

Powell, Anastasia and Nicola Henry (2017) *Sexual Violence in a Digital Age.* London: Palgrave Macmillan.

Rentschler, Carrie. 2014. Rape culture and the feminist politics of social media. *Girlhood Studies* 7 (1): 65–82.

Robehmed, Natalie and Madeline Berg. 2017. Oscar hero to zero: how Harvey Weinstein's power enabled him – and led to his decline. *Forbes*, 13 October.

Roddick, Stephen. 2018. The trouble with Johnny Depp. *Rolling Stone.* 21 June.

Rossetter, Kathryn. 2017. New Dustin Hoffman accuser claims harassment and physical violation on Broadway. *Hollywood Reporter*, 8 December.

Ryzik, Melena, Cara Buckley and Jodi Kantor. 2017. Louis C.K. is accused by 5 women of sexual misconduct. *New York Times*, 9 November.

Schulman, Michael. 2016. How Meryl Streep battled Dustin Hoffman, retooled her role, and won her first Oscar. *Vanity Fair*, April.

Segalov, Michael. 2018. Kevin Spacey's creepy video looks like a cynical attempt at distraction. *Guardian*, 28 December.

Sela-Shayovitz, Revital. 2015. "They are all good boys": the role of the Israeli media in the social construction of gang rape. *Feminist Media Studies* 15 (3): 411–428.

Serisier, Tanya. 2018. *Speaking Out: Feminism, Rape and Narrative Politics*, Cham: Palgrave Macmillan.

Setoodeh, Ramin. 2019. Quentin Tarantino snaps at reporter when asked about Margot Robbie's limited role in "Once Upon a Time in Hollywood". *Variety*, 22 May.

Sills, Sophie, Chelsea Pickens, Karishma Beach, Lloyd Jones, Octavia Calder-Dowe, Paulette Benton-Greig and Nicola Gavey. 2016. Rape culture and social media: young critics and a feminist counterpublic. *Feminist Media Studies* 16 (6): 935–951.

Silverstein, Melissa. 2017. Other stories: Why now is the time for a new movie canon – chosen by women. *Guardian*, 3 November.

Soothill, Keith and Sylvia Walby. 1991. *Sex Crime in the News*. London: Routledge.

Spargo, Chris. 2017. Matt Damon reveals he KNEW Harvey Weinstein harassed Gwyneth Paltrow from his "buddy" Ben Affleck while George Clooney admits mogul was a bully who bragged of bedding stars – but says every industry has this issue. *Mail Online*, 23 October https://www.dailymail.co.uk/news/article-5008429/Matt-Damon-KNEW-Harvey-Weinsten-harassed-Gwyneth-Paltrow.html. Accessed 6 May 2019.

Stamp, Shelley. 2004. "It's a long way to filmland": starlets, screen hopefuls, and extras in early Hollywood. In *American Cinema's Transitional Era: Audiences, Institutions, Practices*, eds. Charlie Keil and Shelley Stamp, 332–351. Berkeley: University of California Press.

Stevens, Dana. 2017. Stories from Slate; just as the election challenged my perception of American, the past week has transformed my whole understanding of Hollywood. *Slate Magazine*, 13 October.

Stolworthy, Jacob. 2017. *30 Rock* joke referenced Harvey Weinstein allegations in 2012. *Independent*, 11 October.

Sullivan, Eric. 2019. "I'm not the morality police": Inside Benjamin Brafman's defense of Harvey Weinstein. *Esquire*, 15 January.

Vincent, Alice. 2017. Did Kevin Spacey hint at his behaviour in his *American Beauty* Oscars speech? *Telegraph*, 31 October.

Weedle, D. 1995. *Straw Dogs:* They want to see brains flying out? *Sight and Sound* 5 (2): 20–25.

Weinstein, Harvey. 2009. Polanksi has served his time and must be freed. *Independent*, 28 September.

Weinstein, Harvey. 2017. Statement. *New York Times*, 5 October.

Zhong, Fan. 2018. What is Kevin Spacey thinking with this evil "Let Me Be Frank" YouTube video? *W.* 24 December. https://www.wmagazine.com/story/kevin-spacey-let-me-be-frank-youtube-video. Accessed 20 May 2019.

Zimmer, Ben. 2017. "Casting couch": The origins of a pernicious Hollywood cliché. *The Atlantic*, 16 October.

Ziv, Stav. 2017. At Oscars Harvey Weinstein thanked more than God, according to 2015 analysis. *Newsweek*, 10 October.

CHAPTER 5

Men in the #MeToo Era

INTRODUCTION

As has been demonstrated throughout this book, whilst #MeToo and Me Too have centred victim/survivors, what the discourse and movement mean *for men* has been a recurring concern in mainstream commentary. This chapter investigates the position of men in the #MeToo era in three contexts: firstly, in relation to men as victim/survivors of sexual abuse (including of female perpetrators); secondly exploring how sexual abuse reports are represented as victimising alleged perpetrators; and finally considering the acknowledged, or credible, male perpetrator as monstrous other. Running across all three sections is a concern with ideas about the exceptionalism of (alleged) perpetrators.

Whilst feminist critics have been interested in the *connections* between "aberrant" and "normal" male behaviour and so in thinking of how abuse can be understood on a continuum of behaviour (Kelly 1988), this analysis is pitted against a cultural context which depends on different forms of distinction, in order to understand male violence as *individual* aberrance. In non-celebrity contexts, the discursive construction of the exceptionalism of male perpetrators—particularly male perpetrators of serial sexual violence and murder (Cameron and Frazer 1987)—can be a means both of celebrification of abusive men *and* of distancing the "aberrant" from the "normal". But how does this work in contexts where the men are *already* marked (and valued) as exceptional in relation to their celebrity or

© The Author(s) 2019
K. Boyle, *#MeToo, Weinstein and Feminism*,
https://doi.org/10.1007/978-3-030-28243-1_5

political status? And (how) can a feminist understanding of the gendered nature of violence help us understand female perpetrators? These are some of the questions I explore in this chapter.

MEN IN #MeToo AS VICTIM/SURVIVORS

It should not be controversial to note that men are also victim/survivors of sexual assault, most often perpetrated by other men. Whilst studies routinely show the majority of rape and sexual assault victims are women, nevertheless there is a sizable minority of male victims (Weiss 2010). For instance, according to the 2011 US National Intimate Partner and Sexual Violence survey, 1.7% of men (compared to 19.3% of women) have been raped, and 23.4% of men (compared to 43.9% women) have experienced other forms of sexual assault (in Mulder et al. 2019).

When it comes to media representation, the picture is contradictory. There is limited evidence that male victims may be *over*-represented in newspaper reporting compared to national statistics (DiBennardo 2018) and that the press are more likely to portray male victims sympathetically, compared to their treatment of female victims (Jamel 2014). However, this is not true for *all* men. In a recent study of representations of sexual predators in the *Los Angeles Times*, Rebecca A. DiBennardo (2018: n.p.) writes, "[t]o the extent that adult male victims fail to live up to masculine, heterosexual ideals, their victim status is devalued similarly to that of adult women." Thus, gay men, for instance, are more likely to be subject to victim-blaming discourses (Davies and Rogers 2006: 371–2).

How has this played out in the #MeToo era? In the early days of October 2017, when the Weinstein story dominated the news agenda, actor and former NFL star Terry Crews came forward with his experience of being groped by an initially unnamed male film executive (@terrycrews 10 October 2017).[1] Crews shared his experience *before* Milano's #MeToo tweet, but he was subsequently embraced by/embraced the #MeToo discourse and, indeed, was one of the "silence breakers" featured in *Time*'s Person of the Year story (see Chap. 2). Importantly, Crews' testimony drew attention to the racialised dynamics of silence, noting that—as a "240lbs. Black Man"—he feared that in speaking out he would be recast as the perpetrator who "stomps out Hollywood Honcho". The extent to which both race and gender combine to encourage a "himpathetic" (Manne 2018a) response to perpetrators is something I explore in the next section. In contrast, Crews points to the fact that men occupying the victim/survivor position can face a "credibility conundrum" (Jordan 2004). The forms of scrutiny may be different for male victim/survivors than their female counterparts (Chap. 4), but their credibility is still established in relation to their ability to occupy gender norms (Weiss 2010; Javaid 2016). For a "240lbs Black Man"—and, specifically, a 240lbs Black former *sportsman*—to speak from the position of victim/survivor upsets gendered and racialised norms around male invulnerability, power and strength.

In this context, it is perhaps not accidental that the male victims/survivors who have achieved a degree of media prominence *as* victims/survivors in the #MeToo moment have been men who are marginalised in relation to race and/or sexuality. Anthony Rapp, who spoke out about Kevin Spacey, for example, is an out gay man, as is Nimrod Reitman who pursued a claim against New York University academic Avital Ronell. As sexual assault is discursively constructed as feminising (Weiss 2010; DiBennardo 2018), men who are already outside of hegemonic constructions of masculinity (Connell and Messerschmidt 2005) are arguably more legible as victims.

The extent to which men are recognised in #MeToo is debatable. Milano's original tweet was explicitly addressed to an audience of women, though prominent men engaging with the hashtag describe how women's testimonies enabled their own (Bradley 2018). At the same time, related hashtags such as #HimToo and #MenToo have tried to make men's experiences explicitly visible. Whilst some of this work has genuinely been about male victim/survivors, the extent to which these gender-specific hashtags have been taken up by people *protesting* #MeToo is important to recognise. The logic here seems to be that if men also experience abuse this can't be about gender, and feminists are not only misguided in their critiques but risk victimising men as a result. This makes speaking out more fraught for male victim/survivors who want to position themselves as feminist allies as the language for expressing their experience has been co-opted as part of the backlash *against* #MeToo. This is what happened with #HimToo, a hashtag which had been used by male victim/survivors positioning themselves alongside #MeToo (O'Neil 2018) but went viral during the Senate Judiciary Committee Hearings for Brett Kavanaugh's Supreme Court nomination. In that context, as I discuss in the next section, conservative commentators sought to re-appropriate #HimToo as an expression of solidarity with Kavanaugh, recasting the accused *perpetrator* of sexual assault as the victim.

Whilst #HimToo sought to undermine the feminist and gendered discourse around #MeToo, the feminist analysis that violence is gendered does *not* depend on female victimisation but rather on an understanding of how violence is enacted and understood in relation to gender in a patriarchal context (Kelly 1996a; Boyle 2005: 94–122). For instance, I have argued in relation to the Jimmy Savile case (Boyle 2018a) that his abuse of boys—as well as girls and adult women—was enabled by particular idea(l)s about masculinity which he was seen to embody and which thus rendered his abusive behaviour unproblematic in that it was not widely recognised *as abuse* (see also Chap. 4). How violence functions societally is indivisible from gender. Because we live in a patriarchal society, power is linked to certain kinds of expressions of masculinity, but the intersectional qualities of power mean that it is also possible for some women to hold power over some men, for instance, through racial privilege, class, wealth, workplace status or age. And some women are sexually abusive (towards women as well as other men). Although statistics on the intersections of gender and violence are notoriously imprecise (Walby et al. 2017), some studies find that female perpetrators are involved in up to 46% of sexual assaults against men (Weiss 2010: 284).

The small number of high-profile stories featuring (alleged) female perpetrators in the #MeToo era have been widely interpreted as a potential challenge to the legitimacy of #MeToo, and/or of feminist analysis and activism (e.g. Greenberg 2018; O'Connell 2018). I am thinking in particular of the reports focused on Asia Argento, the actor/director and prominent Weinstein-accuser, and NYU professor Avital Ronell. Much of this coverage reveals a double standard, whereby an allegation against a woman is automatically read as a gender issue—something that can and should tell us about gender relations—which is rarely true of reports involving a male perpetrator. Patrizia Romito makes this point when she notes how *in*frequently the term "male violence" is used, not only in the documents of governments and international organisations but also in feminist activism and scholarship. It is, she notes, "acceptable to talk about violence, but never about male violence" (2008: 5). On the other hand, women accused of violence are typically marked *as women* using phrases that rarely have a commonly used male equivalent (Boyle 2005: 94–122). Whilst writing this passage, for instance, I searched for "male suicide bombers" on Google: the first result I was offered was the Wikipedia entry for "female suicide bombers". This is what Caroline Criado-Perez (2019) identifies as the "default male" principle: the unmarked term is *assumed to* *be* male (whether it is killer, scientist or footballer), but this makes masculinity invisible as a category for analysis. In relation to victimisation, however, a "default female" principle is in operation: victimisation feminises, creating additional challenges for male victim/survivors (Weiss 2010). At the same time, the term "gender" in often taken as a synonym for "women" and in international policy contexts this means that *"gender-based* violence" and "violence *against women"* can be used interchangeably (Boyle 2019). The apparently gender-neutral term "gender" can thus disguise the gendered realities of who is most often doing what to whom (*men's* violence *against women*) whilst simultaneously creating dissonances for male victim/survivors of sexual violence who do not find themselves reflected in the language used.

None of this is to deny that women can also be sexually abusive against men as well as other women. Rather, it is to highlight that the *meaning* of that abuse is differently constructed (Kelly 1996a). In the remainder of this section, I want to briefly address the Ronell story as a means of untangling these issues.

In June 2018, philosopher Brian Leiter published, on his blog, a letter written in response to an NYU sexual harassment investigation into Professor Avital Ronell signed by a number of prominent academics. Whilst the letter as published by Leiter (still in draft form), acknowledged that the signatories did not have access to the confidential dossier about the case, it nevertheless went on to offer an extended intellectual character reference for Ronell, noting her considerable academic achievements and claiming her accuser had waged a "malicious campaign" against her. For the letter writers, Ronell's scholarship, academic achievements and awards were apparently the grounds for special consideration: an academic version of "auteur apologism" (Marghitu 2018).

What made this story remarkable is not only that Ronell is a woman, but that the letter was signed by a number of key figures in feminist and/or queer theory, most notably Judith Butler. Not surprisingly, these comments attracted widespread criticism, including from feminists, though others continued to defend Ronell and malign Reitman (Arnold 2018). Butler herself offered an explanation of the Ronell defence in another letter, published in the *Chronicle of Higher Education* (Butler 2018a), and in a later public statement stated she made a "serious error" in helping to draft the letter, acknowledging the power dynamics between faculty and graduate students which were the context for this case (Butler 2018b). Yet, as far as I am aware, Butler has not apologised publicly to Reitman although she speaks compellingly of making reparations through future work with and for graduate students. Does that matter? To the extent that this leaves unaddressed the *specific* victim-blaming discourses mobilised in relation to Reitman I think it does.

Leiter's publication of the letter, and the mainstream media response it generated, provided further opportunity for critics of #MeToo to expand upon the already-existing narrative of suspicion around feminism (Chap. 2). In publishing the (draft) letter, Leiter commented: "Blaming the victim is apparently OK when the accused in a Title IX proceeding is a feminist literary theorist" (2018). This was then taken up in the press with the *New York Times* asking "What happens to #MeToo when a feminist is the accused?" (Greenberg 2018) and the *MailOnline* identifying Ronell as a "lesbian feminist scholar" (Brantley 2018). This definition of Ronell was, however, disputed by a colleague who described Ronell as having "made no serious contribution to feminist scholarship" (Chu 2018). This was not an evaluative judgement of Ronell's personal politics but rather a statement about the focus of her scholarship, which was not on feminism or primarily within feminist literary theory. Yet, this label stuck, making the Ronell story, and the Argento story which followed quickly after, stories *about* feminism—or, perhaps more accurately, about feminism's perceived excesses and hypocrisies.

The Ronell case, like the others discussed in this book, raises legitimate questions about who is deemed credible as a perpetrator, what perpetrators are understood to represent and how institutions should respond to accusations. Lisa Duggan (2018) suggests that Ronell was marked as a marginal figure within the academy *at least in some respects* (protected by tenure, but vulnerable as a queer, Jewish, female member of faculty), which made her a more suspicious, more easily sacrificed, figure from the point of view of university authorities. The university did not act to protect Ronell's career and reputation as universities have so routinely and problematically done in relation to similarly accused men (Takla 2018). It is not inconsistent with a feminist analysis to note this, nor does it mean that Ronell *should* have been similarly protected: rather it is to (again) call out the double standards which routinely protect men whilst making a gendered spectacle of women. However, we need to be able to make these arguments without at the same time casting doubt on Reitman's veracity (which Duggan does in unnecessary parenthetical comments about Reitman's husband, for instance). Reitman should be granted the same "presumption of innocence" within feminist discourse as other victim/survivors (Waterhouse-Watson 2012).

Of course, some accused men also make more credible perpetrators than others. I will return to these themes in the final section of this chapter when I explore the "othering" of the credible perpetrator, but this discussion of Ronell, alongside my analysis of the early days of the Weinstein coverage in Chap. 2, suggests that linking the perpetrator to feminism *can* be part of the evaluation of credibility. Feminism is presented as part of the problem, not the solution.

Indeed, the pattern I have observed, where the accusations against Ronell and Weinstein were used to ask questions about feminism per se, can also be found in the coverage of Jimmy Bennett's claim of sexual assault by Asia Argento (O'Connell 2018). Here there was an added complication as Argento was (and is) a key figure in the case against Weinstein. Thus, it was not simply Argento's gender and that of her accuser which was presented as a challenge to #MeToo, her prior claims of victimisation (and the broader #MeToo discourse in which they are embedded) were rendered suspect by this development. Inherent in these responses is an assumption that feminist approaches to sexual violence depend on "fixing" the identity of the (female) victim (Mardorossian 2002: 1999). The assumption is that *both* Argento's and Bennett's claims of victimisation cannot be true: if Bennett is telling the truth, then Argento is no longer a credible victim; if Argento is telling the truth about Weinstein, then Bennett must be lying about Argento. Feminism has a long history of engaging with the complexity of victim/survivors who become abusers, but this is completely elided in these responses.

The two accusations against women discussed here echo previous scholarship which has identified a tendency in media reporting of women's violence to present violent women as the *cost* of feminism (Boyle 2005: 97). In this analysis, feminism and feminists hurt men as well as other women (Chap. 2). However, this discourse performs a disservice to male victims, casting them outside of the collective of victim/survivors and harnessing their stories to reactionary ends which ultimately privilege male perpetrators (who are also those most likely to abuse men). The next section demonstrates how alleged perpetrators can also be transformed into victims of a feminism gone too far, focusing on the Brett Kavanaugh case. In this reworking of the continuum (Chap. 3), it is men's injuries—whether as a result of experiencing sexual assault, or losing a job opportunity because of allegedly perpetrating assault—which are linked, thus positioning male perpetrators alongside male victim/survivors.

#HimToo and Himpathy

In September 2018, Donald Trump's nominee to the Supreme Court, Brett Kavanaugh, faced a report (which he vehemently denied) that he attempted to rape Dr Christine Blasey Ford when they were both in high school. After the report was made public (not by Blasey Ford), both Blasey Ford and Kavanaugh gave televised testimony before the Senate Judiciary Committee, the committee charged with investigating Kavanaugh's suitability to sit on the Supreme Court. Almost a year on from the *New York Times*' Weinstein story, the hearings (which ultimately resulted in Kavanaugh's confirmation) were widely re-presented as an outcome of, and perhaps an endpoint for, #MeToo. Not surprisingly, the case generated huge amounts of commentary, not only in legacy media internationally but also on social media, with users declaring support for Blasey Ford (e.g. #BelieveSurvivors, #IBelieveChristineBlaseyFord) or Kavanaugh (#HimToo, #BeersforKavanaugh/ #BeersforBrett). In this section, I am particularly concerned with the expressions of support for Kavanaugh and the ways in which these depend on narratives of male victimisation in the face of feminist excess. There are, as I will demonstrate, echoes here of the 1991 confirmation hearings for Clarence Thomas when Anita Hill testified of her experiences of sexual harassment from Thomas, her boss, but there are also important differences which highlight the importance of race to our understanding of rape and sexual abuse.

At this point, it is worth re-iterating what was at stake in these hearings. Kavanaugh was *not* on trial. Blasey Ford's evidence was given to help determine whether the President's nominee was a suitable candidate for the Supreme Court. A man of immense privilege, Kavanaugh was nevertheless presented, and indeed presented himself (Kavanaugh 2018), as a victim.

#HimToo provides interesting examples of this. Although #HimToo has a longer history (Ellis 2018), including as a way for men to share experiences of sexual victimisation in the context of #MeToo (O'Neil 2018), it is of interest to me for the way in which it constructs a narrative of male victimisation with Kavanaugh at its centre. The hashtag began trending—and caught the attention of my colleague Chamil Rathnayake and me—in the days before Blasey Ford and Kavanaugh testified (Boyle and Rathnayake 2019).[2] Of course, #HimToo was not the only hashtag doing himpathetic work around the hearings. For example, following Kavanaugh's confirmation, the beers hashtags (#BeersForBrett, #BeersForKavanaugh) allowed users—male and female—to express their support for the new Justice by asserting their affinity with his much-mocked testimonial declarations that he "liked beer". This in itself illustrates a double standard around gendered behaviour. Blasey Ford stated that she had only had one beer on the night of the attack, something Trump openly and aggressively mocked her for (Malloy et al. 2018). Blasey Ford was in a no-win situation: as a victim of attempted rape, the consumption of alcohol could have rendered her incredible (Romero-Sánchez et al. 2018: 1054); but—unlike Kavanaugh— she could not use ritual social drinking as a defence. Indeed, although Kavanaugh made a series of statements about his use of alcohol which were convincingly disputed (e.g. Ludington et al. 2018), the beers hashtags suggest that the truthfulness of his testimony mattered less in certain contexts than the sociality of his address. As we will see, despite his privilege, the beer-drinking college-boy turned family-man, became a stand-in for American masculinity rendered newly vulnerable by the fallout from #MeToo.

The Kavanaugh-supportive hashtags—as well as the performance of the President and some of Kavanaugh's supposed Republican interlocutors on the Senate Judiciary Committee—provide a stark example of what Kate Manne (2018a) calls "himpathy". In a commentary on the Kavanaugh case, Manne defines himpathy as, "the inappropriate and disproportionate sympathy powerful men often enjoy in cases of sexual assault, homicide and other misogynistic behaviour". She continues:

> the higher a man rises in the social hierarchy, the more himpathy he tends to attract. Thus, the bulk of our collective care, consideration, respect and nurturing attention is allotted to the most privileged in our society. (Manne 2018b)

The most privileged demand our attention, not least because they are so routinely represented as points of identification that a himpathetic perspective is utterly normalised. At the same time, this means that the most privileged can be re-presented as the most vulnerable, the most prone to malicious victimisation, *precisely because they have the most to lose*. Moreover, as Kavanaugh repeatedly emphasised (e.g. Kavanaugh 2018), an attack on him was an attack on his *good name*, a name shared with his parents, wife and daughters.[3] Blasey Ford's accusations were not only an attack on (Brett) Kavanaugh but also an attack on *the* Kavanaughs as exemplars of the white, upper-middle class, heterosexual family unit. This allowed Blasey Ford's testimony to be re-constructed as an attack *on women*.

My work with Chamil Rathnayake on the #HimToo hashtag demonstrates that conservative women were at the centre of the #HimToo network up until Kavanaugh's nomination was confirmed (Boyle and Rathnayake 2019). These women were often speaking *as mothers* and/or as fearful of the implications of accusation for "*our*" men (fathers, brothers, husbands and particularly sons). Notably, although support for Trump has been famously low among Black women (and highest among white women), the most prominent actor in our #HimToo sample from this period was a female African American political activist. It would be a mistake to generalise from the Twitter-dominance of this highly atypical figure; nevertheless, this does suggest that party-affiliation was key to himpathetic judgements of Kavanaugh, something our data supports. In terms of the overall arguments of this book, this is arguably of a piece with discussions of value in Chap. 4 and in relation to Avital Ronell, above: victim/survivors' statements about their experiences of sexual assault are weighed against the cultural, social and political value of (alleged) perpetrators. The judgement is not *did it happen?* Rather, there is an earlier judgement about the relative importance of the alleged perpetrator and victim/survivor, and the potential damage *to the alleged perpetrator* of the claim that it did.

In relation to #HimToo, himpathetic judgements were primarily based on affective and familial connections, as well as on ideas about character, standing and morality. As Manne (2018a) notes, the structure of sympathy places the (usually white, wealthy, heterosexual) man at its centre so that the starting point in this discourse is what sexual assault allegations mean for the men accused (Sela-Shayovitz 2015). Whilst Manne (not writing about Kavanaugh specifically), suggests that in cases of violence himpathy works by "effectively making him into the victim of his own crimes" (2018a: 210), I would argue that, certainly in the #MeToo era, himpathetic responses suggest not that it is the crimes which victimise the (alleged) perpetrator, but rather the feminists who name them *as* crimes. This is about "good" (and *known*) men, versus typically generic and anonymous (and, hence, suspicious) women, or unjust institutions dominated by "liberals" and dedicated to the demise of the American family.

In our work on #HimToo, Rathnayake and I also identified that supporters sought to assert Kavanaugh's vulnerability by allying him with African American males (Boyle and Rathnayake 2019) and I want to expand on this potentially counter-intuitive point here. The obvious link is with Justice Clarence Thomas, now one of Kavanaugh's immediate colleagues on the Supreme Court, who faced sexual harassment allegations during his confirmation hearings in 1991. Thomas is an African American whose nomination was largely opposed by African Americans *prior* to Anita Hill's testimony given his consistent self-presentation as a "colour-blind" candidate and his failure to advocate for African Americans (Morrison 1992a). However, in the wake of Hill's sexual harassment testimony, Thomas's description of the hearings as a "high-tech lynching" generated support for Thomas on the (white, male) committee as well as among many African Americans. Of course, this also meant *dis*believing an African American woman (Hill) who was subject to horrendous racialised and sexualised caricature and abuse. As many of the contributors to Toni Morrison's 1992 collection on the Hill/Thomas hearings argue, Black women's victimisation is so routinely ignored that when Thomas drew on a recognisable history of white violence against Black men he was able to recast himself as the victim and Hill was no longer legible *as* Black (Morrison 1992a). Rather Hill was recast as a representative of feminists "hopelessly out of touch with the real women of America" (Ross 1992: 44), a phrase that also finds powerful echoes in many #HimToo responses.

It is important to note the very different ways in which Blasey Ford and Hill were treated during their respective testimonies and in their widespread coverage. As my discussion of #HimToo suggests—and as the threats to Blasey Ford which continued for months after her testimony starkly demonstrate (Ryan 2018)—Blasey Ford was, like Hill, called a liar and explicitly re-victimised through the process of speaking out. However, it is notable that the Senate Judiciary Committee on the whole took a very different approach to Blasey Ford, and refrained from direct attacks during her testimony. Blasey Ford was widely deemed credible, if mistaken. Kavanaugh's own testimony did not consistently denigrate Blasey Ford and, indeed, suggested the need to extend compassion to a woman so confused as to make this accusation. In contrast, Hill's credibility was consistently in doubt: she was "out of place" in the hearings, too sexual, too aggressive, too composed, too explicit and factual in her testimony, not emotional enough. Most importantly, as a Black woman—and a conservative, educated Black woman at that – she was not *legible* in existing narratives (Crenshaw 1992). As Nell Irvin Painter argues, Hill "chose not to make herself into a symbol Americans could recognize, and as a result she seemed to disappear, a feat reserved for black women who are educated and thus doubly hard to see" (Painter 1992: 210). One effect of the Kavanaugh hearings has been that Hill's appalling treatment in front of the committee has received renewed attention. Whilst there is justifiable concern that the lessons of Hill's experience have still not been learned (Crenshaw 2018), the behaviour of the Senators—in particular Joe Biden, who is seeking the Democratic Presidential nomination for 2020—has been under heightened scrutiny.[4]

Re-reading Morrison's collection on the 1991 hearings in the wake of Kavanaugh, I was struck by her introductory claim that "an accusation of such weight as sexual misconduct would probably have disqualified a white candidate on its face". Whilst this clearly no longer holds, Morrison's argument about why these charges would have been disqualifying for a white man in 1991 are worth returning to as I try to make sense of the kinship of vulnerability between Kavanaugh and Thomas which emerged in the #HimToo data. Morrison argues:

> in a racialized and race-conscious society, standards are changed, facts marginalized, repressed, and the willingness to air such charges, actually to debate them, outweighed the seemliness of a substantive hearing because the actors were black. (Morrison 1992b: xvii)

Racialised and sexualised notions of Black bodies made Thomas and Hill legitimate objects of spectacle and investigation. Morrison does not ignore that white men in power have routinely committed these kinds of assaults (clearly, they have). Rather she draws our attention to the way that white men's violence is invisible as such. White men could not bear the weight of this kind of investigation because, as the normative subjects of narrative, to render them object would be to compromise their power in an untenable way.

From Morrison's collection, it is clear that whilst Thomas was able to call on a history of the literal lynching of African American males to defend himself against Hill's testimony, this was only credible to his white, male interlocutors precisely because—as a conservative with a long history of opposing civil rights measures—he was *not* perceived to embody "blackness" up until this point (Morrison 1992a). Supporting Thomas was thus a *posture* of anti-racism which did not require actual anti-racist work and this is arguably central to Thomas's appeal to Kavanaugh and his supporters. Thomas establishes a powerful precedent: for the Senate Judiciary Committee to then treat Kavanaugh "differently" could open up a charge of racism, that he was not treated as fairly as his Black predecessor. Here it is white women who are the imagined perpetrators, allowing white men's role in lynching to be rewritten to create an affinity between men of different racial groups on the basis of (white) women's allegations. (That this depended, and still depends, on a denial of Anita Hill's racial identity is a recurring theme in Morrison's collection.) This also underscores the sense that in the #MeToo era no man—not even a white, God-fearing, family-loving one— is safe from feminist excess.

In the #HimToo data, it is also African American men who are mobilised as warnings of feminism gone too far. Thus, Kavanaugh and the nascent #HimToo "movement" are not only linked to Thomas but also with: Brian Banks, a footballer wrongly convicted of rape; Herman Cain, whose campaign for the 2012 Republican Presidential nomination was derailed by reports of sexual harassment; and, staggeringly, Emmett Till, the 14-year old boy brutally murdered in Mississippi in 1955 for allegedly offending a white woman. These moves establish continuities between the accused perpetrator and actual Black male victims of physical and sexual violence. This only makes sense if you accept that Emmett Till's loss of life is on the same plane as Clarence Thomas or Brett Kavanaugh's potential loss of a lucrative job opportunity. But in a himpathetic world view this *does* make sense because the question we are invited to ask is *what does it mean for him?* That Kavanaugh's (and, to an extent, Thomas's) privilege is such that his greatest fear is the loss of his name and reputation (his physical safety is not at risk, nor is his material advantage) then this is what a himpathetic response asks us to care most about. And, as discussed in Chap. 4, his loss can be presented as *our* loss, because of his cultural, or in this case social and political, value.

Of course, the Kavanaugh hearings also generated much explicitly feminist commentary both on social and legacy media. But in crucial ways, the himpathetic response won out: Kavanaugh was, after all, confirmed to the Supreme Court, a lifetime position which will give him power over important decisions, not least those affecting the rights of marginalised Americans. At the same time, again paralleling events in 1991/1992, Kavanaugh's confirmation was also a precipitating factor—along with Trump's election and #MeToo—in the election of record numbers of women in the 2018 midterms. As I have argued throughout this book, this remains a profoundly contradictory time for feminist politics, activism and visibility, and Kavanaugh is a cautionary reminder of the resilience of white male power, even as critical responses to the hearings and his confirmation demonstrate the continued resurgence of resistance.

If Kavanaugh was an *in*credible perpetrator who could credibly, if temporarily, adopt a victim position to re-assert his entitlement to himpathetic treatment, what is it that allows others—like Weinstein or Savile—to be (finally) seen as credible perpetrators, largely *un*deserving of himpathy? It is to this question that I turn my attention in the final section.

CREDIBLE PERPETRATORS

The celebrity men whose reputations have been most spectacularly and overwhelmingly negatively impacted by sexual abuse allegations—in terms of both criminal justice and popular opinion—are rarely men like Kavanaugh who are at the height of their fame and power. When the Jimmy Savile story finally gained traction Savile was already dead, and it is doubtful that the *Leaving Neverland* (dir. Dan Reed 2018) documentary could have achieved such a sympathetic hearing during Michael Jackson's lifetime. In the UK, celebrity figures who have been jailed for sexual abuse *and* widely demonised as a result—Gary Glitter, Rolf Harris, Stuart Hall, Max Clifford—have rarely been in their prime. These cases provide striking contrasts with others against still successful sportsmen (Ched Evans, Adam Johnson, the Belfast rugby rape trial) who tend to receive more himpathetic coverage with concerns routinely raised about *their* wasted potential.

This is a useful extension of my arguments about cultural value in Chap. 4: when it comes to young men in particular, their value can lie in their potential as well as (or even in place of) their existing achievements. Among the most notorious examples of this in recent years are the case of the blond-haired, blue-eyed swimmer-with-Olympic-potential, Brock Turner, who raped an unconscious woman but received minimal jail time despite being found guilty; and the Steubenville high-school rapists, stars of the football team who received much community support. These are by no means unique cases (Waterhouse-Watson 2013; Benedict 1997). The lost potential of victim/survivors is rarely part of the broader discourse, though Turner's victim/survivor fought hard to make her story, *her* lost potential, matter against a context where his swimming times were widely reported alongside initial accounts of the rape (Doe 2016).

Potential was clearly not at stake in relation to Weinstein, even though he tried to make his *political* potential as a thorn-in-the-side of the National Rifle Association part of his initial statement (Weinstein 2017). The older a perpetrator is, the less wasted potential seems to be at stake in media coverage (unless, perhaps, he is nominated to the Supreme Court or running for President). However, I want to argue that this is not just about potential, but rather the extent to which the perpetrator can be convincingly re-constructed as an outsider. A himpathetic engagement depends on a certain *fit* between the reputation or potential of the individual and the priorities and values of the institution, community or even nation.

It is worth briefly reflecting on the media treatment of Kevin Spacey in this context as, despite arguably still being at the height of his acting career, he has been widely (though by no means uniformly) condemned since Anthony Rapp went public. That the allegations against Spacey involved children is only part of the story here: footballer Adam Johnson and director Roman Polanski were, after all, convicted of sexual activity with (girl) children. That the allegations against Spacey involved multiple boy children seems to be the significant factor here, cementing a homophobic association of homosexuality and paedophilia to enable the re-construction of Spacey as monstrous other. Nevertheless, the ambivalence which characterises some of the online responses to Spacey, discussed in Chap. 4, demonstrate that there remains a continued pleasurable investment in the actor and his roles which hinge on abuse being re-presented as risk-taking, amoral masculinity.

Of course, the *scale* of the alleged abuse, the number of victim/survivors coming forward, and the quality of the investigative journalism are all important in understanding why the reports of sexual abuse finally "stuck" to Weinstein—as to Spacey—in public opinion in 2017. Yet, as established elsewhere in this book, multiple rumours surrounded Weinstein for years to no significant effect, so this isn't the whole story. Weinstein's own declining position of power, artistic and financial, within the film industry was also an important context for the eventual credibility of his accusers. By the time of Kantor and Twohey's story, Weinstein's declining significance had been documented for some time and he was no longer able to control media coverage in the way he had done during his heyday (Auletta 2002; Perren 2012).

However, it is also notable that Weinstein was always constructed, and indeed often sought to construct himself, as a partial outsider to the industry that made him, and that he made. Weinstein's self-construction as an outsider could, at times, be a way of insisting on his exceptionalism. For instance, in a lengthy 2002 profile in the *New Yorker*, Weinstein claimed outsider status as a means of asserting his cinephilic tastes and knowledge in an industry where commerce rules (Auletta 2002). In an interview with CNN early in 2017, his self-identification as an underdog was equally integral to his construction of discerning taste, creating affinities with the leading characters of some of his most successful films of recent years: *The King's Speech* (dir. Tom Hooper 2010), *The Imitation Game* (dir. Morten Tyldum 2014) and *Lion* (dir. Garth Davis 2016).[5] As with Kavanaugh or Thomas, his strategic self-identification with victimised and/or marginalised characters is a means of disavowing or re-interpreting his own problematic behaviour. In both these pieces, Weinstein-the-cineaste and Weinstein-the-underdog are placed alongside Weinstein-the-bully, but this allows his bullying behaviour to be rewritten as evidence of passion *on behalf of the marginalised* (whether that is marginalised characters or artists whose vision is subordinated to commerce). Of course, this is a very expansive understanding of marginalisation, where even the British King can heroically overcome the odds.

At the same time, this chimes with the story that is told of Weinstein's own history, a version of the American dream whereby a Jewish boy can "climb out of the Queens shtetl where he grew up" (Biskind 2004: 54), learn to love foreign and independent film (ibid. 61), and hence make his fortune. Weinstein's Jewish identity is repeatedly—though often implicitly—marked in discussions of his critical and commercial success prior to October 2017. Renov and Brook (2017: ix) note that the term "mogul", frequently used in relation to Harvey Weinstein, is of anti-semitic origin. In a discussion of the studio-bosses of classical Hollywood, Brook expands on this point:

> The term mogul itself, derived from the word "Mongol" and coined specifically for the immigrant studio bosses, referred pejoratively to their "alleged Asiatic [read: alien] provenance and appearance, perceived boorish [read: uncivilised] behaviour, and admittedly aggressive [read: unscrupulous] business practices." (Brook 2017: 5)

The use of "mogul" in relation to Weinstein—and, indeed, his own apparent embrace of the term—thus speaks in complex ways to the history of Jewish men in Hollywood, all at once suggesting his outsider status and control, his uncivilised and unscrupulous behaviour and his success. There is much more thinking to be done about how Weinstein's Jewishness is central to the ease with which he is othered, not least because it speaks to this long and complex history and the ways in which the "moguls" have come to represent power, control, success but also amorality, depravity and excess (Brook 2017).

Weinstein's outsider status is also repeatedly *aesthetically* marked. For instance, the *New Yorker* story mentioned above is entitled "Beauty and the beast" and makes repeated reference to Weinstein's physical bulk, all "two hundred and fifty pounds," of it (Auletta 2002). He is "a fearsome sight – his eyes dark and glowering, his fleshy face unshaved, his belly jutting forward half a foot or so ahead of his body". His size is rendered cartoonish as we are told that in his recently remodelled office "everything in it seems too small for the large man who occupies it". But physical bulk is not the only way in which Weinstein is marked as excessive: his temper as well as his body is seen to exceed boundaries, to "burst" out. As I noted in Chap. 4, Weinstein's aesthetic "otherness" in the groomed world of Hollywood was something which made him easier to mark as monstrous when the *New York Times* story broke, though this also has implications for victim/survivors: the implicit (and sometimes explicit) question is how could they *not* know just by *looking* at him? This is one of the central appeals of monsterising sexual abusers, namely the way it allows us to draw a line between the "good" and "bad" men, even at a glance, thus leaving hegemonic constructions of masculinity largely untroubled. The prettier boys of Hollywood have not, on the whole, been given the same treatment, as my discussion of Johnny Depp in Chap. 4 suggests.

There are clear parallels between Harvey Weinstein and, in a UK context, Jimmy Savile. Although very much a figure of the establishment in terms of access and influence, Savile's heavy regional accent, working-class background, and outlandish dress marked him as "other" in a BBC of received pronunciation and Oxbridge graduates. Savile cultivated a deliberately outlandish persona and, as he aged, his youthful but out-of-date costuming (tracksuits, string vests, medallion), flyaway hair and poor dentistry all made him a markedly odd and physically unattractive figure (Boyle 2018b). When the sexual assault claims against him finally stuck, he was fairly easily re-constructed as the monstrous "other", the paedophile (Kitzinger 1999; Kelly 1996b). As with Weinstein, this re-construction allowed Savile to be held at a distance, even (or especially) as questions of institutional complicity in enabling his decades of abuse were explored. As I have argued elsewhere, this also meant that the *gendered* lessons which might have been learned were largely effaced (Boyle 2018a). Savile represented no one other than himself and, like Weinstein, became a yardstick against which subsequent stories of celebrity abuse could be measured. This is beautifully captured in the Channel 4 drama *National Treasure* (2016) where the accused comedian, Paul Finchley (played by Robbie Coltrane) exclaims in horror: "They think I'm fucking Jimmy Savile". The fact that he is patently *not* Jimmy Savile (he wears suits, is married, has a daughter, lives in luxury, is "respectable") is mobilised in his defence.

These celebrity examples speak to a broader context where other men's crimes are deployed by abusive men as a kind of mitigation: they are not "as bad as" men who have committed more extreme crimes. For instance, in his work with abusive men, Jeff Hearn (1998) notes how their repeated use of the word "just" works to establish an exculpating hierarchy of seriousness. When a hierarchy, rather than a continuum, is in operation, men's violence can be more easily normalised and excused. Monsters work to (re)define the norm: instead of seeing different kinds of male violence as connected, the figure of the monstrous other allows "normal" male behaviour to go unremarked. In this sense, Weinstein and Savile are convenient figures as they are so easily marked as "other". That this is possible even for men who have enjoyed such power, privilege and prestige *within* the establishment, highlights how much more precarious the position is for men without that power. As feminist scholars have consistently noted, allegations of sexual violence—whether in criminal justice or media contexts—are much more likely to "stick" to men who do not conform to hegemonic notions of masculinity (Boyle 2005: 68–73).

Writing in the aftermath of the New Delhi rape and murder case, Benedict (2013, n.p.) additionally notes that "*why* the men do it" is only considered when the rapes take place in "other" cultures: "as soon as we look at rape among our own, whether civilian or military, this perspective is entirely neglected. Instead, we ask questions about the victim" (also Durham 2015). However, in the context of my discussion here, I would place the emphasis differently and, following Romito (2008), note that "why the *men* do it" is the more challenging question, demanding an understanding the role of gender inequality and hegemonic masculinity in perpetuating male violence against women. If men accused of rape or other forms of sexual violence are from minority communities or "other" cultures they are much more likely to be portrayed as representatives of those communities than as *men*. In contrast, when white men are the perpetrators, the work of "othering", which I have discussed in this section, functions to keep them at a distance from categories of race and gender whilst focusing on questions of individual deviance. A number of studies have demonstrated this process by comparing the coverage of similar cases involving different categories of perpetrators, for instance, so-called honour killings within minority ethnic communities compared to family murder/suicides perpetrated by white men in Canada (Shier and Shor 2016), or recent "sex grooming" cases in the UK involving Asian male perpetrators compared to earlier cases in the same city involving stories of ritual child abuse within white families (Salter and Dagistanli 2015).

This demonstrates a marked reluctance to understand men's violence against women structurally and consider what men (as a group) stand to gain from violence against women. Focusing on individual perpetrators or alleged perpetrators—as I have done in this chapter and, indeed, throughout the book—can exacerbate this problem, and contribute to the construction of the perpetrator as a unique and exceptional case. However, by placing this discussion of Weinstein, Kavanaugh, Savile and others in a broader context informed by feminist scholarship on representations of male perpetrators, the individual monster begins to look like a decidedly generic figure. In relation to celebrity perpetrators—and, indeed, to perpetrators whose crimes render them celebrities, such as serial killers (Boyle and Reburn 2015)—this can provide a way of puncturing that narrative of exceptionalism whilst also reminding us of who and what is let off the hook in the stories we tell about himpathetic victim/perpetrators and monstrous others.

Conclusion

The feminist understanding of the gendered nature of violence remains profoundly threatening in a patriarchal context where the maleness of male violence is both taken for granted and invisible. In contrast, the mainstream portrayal of female violence is routinely about gender, thus creating implicit and explicit links between female violence and feminism. The contemporary examples explored in this chapter demonstrate the persistence of these patterns in the #MeToo era, whilst also highlighting some of the ways in which representations of male victimisation and perpetration are shaped by race, ethnicity and class.

This supports the argument developed across this book that whilst #MeToo as a discourse is fundamentally about gender relations and contemporary understandings of feminism, mainstream mediations of feminism and feminist issues remain profoundly contradictory and ambivalent. That Burke's Me Too is part of a longer and continuing *movement* against men's violence against women is too rarely acknowledged in the popular re-constructions of #MeToo with which this book has been primarily concerned. This does not mean that #MeToo has not done feminist work. But #MeToo is not the sum of feminist work in this area, and for the discursive activism with which is it associated to facilitate enduring material and political change it is important to connect with this wider feminist activism, knowledge and research.

In the time I have been researching and writing this book, the reach of #MeToo has continued to extend across different industries and countries, while the criminal cases against some of the most prominent figures in these pages, including Harvey Weinstein and Kevin Spacey, are ongoing. The backlash has also grown and whilst I have focused on instances of backlash which have hinged on unruly, older feminists (Chap. 2) and prominent US men, from Matt Damon (Chap. 4) to Brett Kavanaugh (this chapter), the local and regional character of the backlash will require future research. Unsurprisingly, feminist research on #MeToo is also proliferating (as demonstrated in the references throughout this book) and this work will help to thicken our understanding of specific uses, understandings of, and responses to the hashtag.

As such, it seems premature to offer a "conclusion" to this book. Instead, what this book offers is a passionate argument for the advantage of understanding #MeToo historically and contextually, alongside some examples of how this work might proceed. This means paying attention to the relationships of on and offline, representation and action, and the different functions each can fulfil for feminist activism. It also means acknowledging that the history of feminism is still being written as the movement endures and adapts. There are tensions and disagreements within feminist communities—as well as beyond them—on the issues discussed in this book. As such, there remains much more work to be done on how #MeToo has played out in different local, regional and national contexts, as well as across different platforms, and whether or how this has impacted the work of long-standing feminist organisations working in the field of men's violence against women. As I stated in the Introduction, by insisting that we cannot conflate the media with the movement, this book offers a model—particularly, but by no means exclusively, for those of us in media disciplines—of how we might (re)integrate and learn from decades of feminist activism and interdisciplinary scholarship on men's violence against women. #MeToo has offered a spectacularly high-profile example which brings many of the central concerns of feminist thinking on men's violence against women into focus, from the function of personal testimony in political and media discourse (Chap. 2), to the gendered and systemic nature of men's violence against women in patriarchal contexts (Chaps. 2 and 3), to the ways in which the culture creates a conducive context for that violence (Chap. 4) placing the lives, work and values of (white) perpetrators at the centre of our universe (Chap. 5). Whilst there is still a long way to go, I want to retain some of the optimism as well as the urgency and anger of the contemporary moment, the sense that #MeToo has been genuinely transformational for some women and men and—if we heed the lessons of the past and learn with the intersectional activism of the present—can still be genuinely transformational of cultures, practices and institutions.

The goal remains to eradicate the need for future generations to have to say #MeToo.

NOTES

1. Crews later named his assailant as agent Adam Venit (Zacharek et al. 2017).
2. Our paper, #HimToo and the networking of misogyny in the age of #MeToo, identifies two key moments in the life of the #HimToo hashtag: the Kavanaugh-supportive engagement which surrounded the hearings, and the satirical, critical use of the hashtag which dominated following his confirmation. By the end of October, we found the hashtag had largely died out. Our paper maps the life of the hashtag (using a data set of 277,856 #HimToo tweets) using both social network analysis (to understand actor centrality and connectivity) combined with a qualitative analysis of the tweets themselves (to understand how it engaged with #MeToo and the Kavanaugh case). In this chapter, I am primarily concerned with the himpathetic Kavanaugh-supportive engagement and my analysis draws on the 112,169 tweets we gathered from 25 September to 5 October 2017.
3. I am grateful to Melody House for this observation.
4. *Intersectionality Matters* (podcast): Episode 4 – The anatomy of an apology, 7 June 2019. https://soundcloud.com/intersectionality-matters/ep-4-the-anatomy-of-an-apology. Accessed 8 June 2019.
5. Weinstein CNN interview: https://www.youtube.com/watch?v=yVUMeLsvzjw. Accessed 6 June 2019.

REFERENCES

Arnold, Amanda. 2018. What's going on with Avital Ronell, the prominent theorist accused of harassment? *The Cut*. 21 August. https://www.thecut.com/2018/08/avital-ronell-professor-accused-of-harassment-what-to-know.html. Accessed 3 June 2019.

Auletta, Ken. 2002. Beauty and the beast. *New Yorker*, 8 December.

Benedict, Jeff. 1997. *Public Heroes, Private Felons: Athletes and Crimes Against Women*. Boston: Northeastern University Press.

Benedict, Helen. 2013. Covering rape responsibly. *WMC: Women Under Siege* (Blog). 1 February. http://www.womensmediacenter.com/women-under-siege/covering-rape-responsibly. Accessed 20 May 2019.

Biskind, Peter. 2004. *Down and Dirty Pictures: Miramax, Sundance, and the Rise of Independent Film*. New York: Simon & Schuster.

Boyle, Karen. 2005. *Media and Violence: Gendering the Debates*. London: Sage.

Boyle, Karen. 2018a. Hiding in plain sight: gender, sexism and press coverage of the Jimmy Savile case. *Journalism Studies* 19 (11): 1562–1578.

Boyle, Karen. 2018b. Television and/as testimony in the Jimmy Savile case. *Critical Studies in Television* 13 (4): 387–404.

Boyle, Karen. 2019. What's in a name? Theorising the inter-relationships of gender and violence. *Feminist Theory* 20 (1): 19–68.

Boyle, Karen and Chamil Rathnayake. 2019. #HimToo and the networking of misogyny in the age of #MeToo. *Feminist Media Studies*. DOI: https://doi.org/10.1080/14680777.2019.1661868

Boyle, Karen and Jenny Reburn. 2015. Portrait of a serial killer: Intertextuality and gender in the portrait film. *Feminist Media Studies* 15 (2): 192–207.

Bradley, Linda. 2018. "I was terrified, and I was humiliated.": #MeToo's male accusers, one year later. *Vanity Fair*, 4 October.

Brantley, Kayla. 2018. Lesbian feminist scholar, 66, is SUSPENDED by NYU after sending racy texts and "inappropriately touching" her 34-year-old married gay former doctoral student. *MailOnline*, 14 August. https://www.dailymail.co.uk/news/article-6057541/World-renowned-female-NYU-professor-facing-MeToo-moment.html. Accessed 10 June 2019.

Brook, Vincent. 2017. Still an empire of their own: how Jews remain atop a reinvented Hollywood. In *From Shtetl to Stardom: Jews and Hollywood. (An Annual Review of the Casden Institute for the Study of the Jewish Role in American Life: Volume 14.)* Eds. Michael Renov and Vincent Brook, 3–21. West Lafayette: Purdue University Press.

Butler, Judith. 2018a. Judith Butler explains letter in support of Avital Ronell. *Chronicle of Higher Education*, 20 August.

Butler, Judith. 2018b. My life, your life: equality and the philosophy of non-violence (part 2). Public lecture. University of Glasgow. 2 October.

Cameron, Deborah and Elizabeth Frazer. 1987. *The Lust to Kill: A Feminist Investigation of Sexual Murder*. Cambridge: Polity.

Chu, Andrea Long. 2018. I worked with Avital Ronell. I believe her accuser. *Chronicle of Higher Education*, 20 August.

Connell, R.W. and Messerschmidt, James W. 2005. Hegemonic masculinity: rethinking the concept. *Gender and Society* 19 (6): 829–259.

Crenshaw, Kimberlé. 1992. Whose story is it anyway? Feminist and antiracist appropriations of Anita Hill. In *Race-ing Justice, En-Gendering Power: Essays on Anita Hill, Clarence Thomas, and the Construction of Social Reality*. Ed. Toni Morrison, 402–440. New York: Pantheon.

Crenshaw, Kimberlé. 2018. We still haven't learned from Anita Hill's testimony. *New York Times*, 27 September.

Criado-Perez, Caroline. 2019. *Invisible Women: Exposing Data Bias in a World Designed for Men*. London: Chatto & Windus.

Davies, Michelle and Paul Rogers. 2006. Perceptions of male victims in depicted sexual assaults: a review of the literature. *Aggression and Violent Behavior* 11: 367–377.

DiBennardo, Rebecca A. 2018. Ideal victims and monstrous offenders: how the news media represent sexual predators. *Socius: Sociological Research for a Dynamic World*. 5 October. https://journals.sagepub.com/doi/full/10.1177/2378023118802512. Accessed 3 June 2019.

Doe, Emily. 2016. Victim impact statement. https://www.sccgov.org/sites/da/newsroom/newsreleases/Documents/B-Turner%20VIS.pdf. Accessed 6 June 2019.

Duggan, Lisa. 2018. The full catastrophe. *Bully Bloggers* (Blog). 18 August. https://bullybloggers.wordpress.com/2018/08/18/the-full-catastrophe/. Accessed 3 June 2019.

Durham, Meenakshi Gigi. 2015. Scene of the crime: news discourse or rape in India and the geopolitics of sexual assault. *Feminist Media Studies* 15 (2): 175–191.

Ellis, Emma Grey. 2018. How #HimToo became the anti #MeToo of the Kavanaugh hearings. *Wired*, 27 September. https://www.wired.com/story/brett-kavanaugh-hearings-himtoo-metoo-christine-blasey-ford/. Accessed 27 November 2018.

Greenberg, Zoe. 2018. What happens to #MeToo when a feminist is the accused? *New York Times*, 13 August.

Hearn, Jeff. 1998. *The Violences of Men*. London & Thousand Oaks: Sage.

Jamel, Joanna. 2014. Do the print-based media provide a gender-biased representation of male rape victims. *Internet Journal of Criminology* https://docs.wix-static.com/ugd/b93dd4_9378310f905442eaa439aba1032586a5.pdf. Accessed 3 June 2019.

Javaid, Aliraza. 2016. Feminism, masculinity and male rape: bringing male rape "out of the closet". *Journal of Gender Studies* 25 (3): 283–293.

Jordan, Jan. 2004. *The Word of a Woman? Police, Rape and Belief*. Hampshire: Palgrave Macmillan.

Kavanaugh, Brett. 2018. I am an independent, impartial judge. *Wall Street Journal*, 4 October.

Kelly, Liz. 1988. *Surviving Sexual Violence*. Cambridge: Polity.

Kelly, Liz. 1996a. When does the speaking profit us?: reflections on the challenges of developing feminist perspectives on abuse and violence by women. In *Women, Violence and Male Power*, eds. Marianne Hester, Liz Kelly and Jill Radford, 34–49. Buckingham: Open University Press.

Kelly, Liz. 1996b. Weasel words: paedophiles and the cycle of abuse. *Trouble and Strife* 33: 44–49.

Kitzinger, Jenny. 1999. The ultimate neighbour from hell?: stranger danger and the media representation of "paedophilia". In *Social Policy, the Media and Misrepresentation*, ed. Bob Franklin, 207–221. London: Routledge.

Leiter, Brian. 2018. Blaming the victim is apparently OK when the accused in a Title IX proceeding is a feminist literary theorist. *Leiter Reports: A Philosophy Blog*, 10 June. https://leiterreports.typepad.com/blog/2018/06/blaming-the-victim-is-apparently-ok-when-the-accused-is-a-feminist-literary-theorist.html. Accessed 31 May 2019.

Ludington, Charles, Lynne Brookes and Elizabeth Swisher. 2018. We were Brett Kavanaugh's drinking buddies. We don't think he should be confirmed. No one should be able to lie their way onto the Supreme Court. *Washington Post* (Blogs), 5 October.

Malloy, Allie, Kate Sullivan and Jeff Zeleny. 2018. Trump mocks Christine Blasey Ford's testimony, tells people to "think of your sons". *CNN*. 3 October. https://edition.cnn.com/2018/10/02/politics/trump-mocks-christine-bla-sey-ford-kavanaugh-supreme-court/index.html. Accessed 5 June 2019.

Manne, Kate. 2018a. *Down Girl: The Logic of Misogyny*. New York: Oxford University Press.

Manne, Kate. 2018b. Brett Kavanaugh and America's "himpathy" reckoning. *New York Times*, 26 September.

Mardorossian, Carine M. 2002. Towards a new feminist theory of rape. *Signs: Journal of Women in Culture and Society*. 27 (3): 743–775.

Marghitu, Stefania. 2018. "It's just art": auteur apologism in the post-Weinstein era. *Feminist Media Studies* 18 (3): 491–494.

Morrison, Toni. ed. 1992a. *Race-ing Justice, En-Gendering Power: Essays on Anita Hill, Clarence Thomas, and the Construction of Social Reality*. New York: Pantheon.

Morrison, Toni. 1992b. Introduction: Friday on the Potomac. In *Race-ing Justice, En-Gendering Power: Essays on Anita Hill, Clarence Thomas, and the Construction of Social Reality*. Ed. Toni Morrison, vii–xxx. New York: Pantheon

Mulder, Eva, Antony Pemberton and Ad J.J.M. Vingerhoets. 2019. The feminising effect of sexual violence in third-party perceptions of male and female victims. *Sex Roles*. DOI: https://doi.org/10.1007/s11199-019-01036-w.

O'Connell, Jennifer. 2018. #HimToo: What happens if the aggressor is a woman? *Irish Times*, 25 August.

O'Neil, Luke. 2018. #HimToo: how an attempt to criticise #MeToo went delight-fully wrong. *Guardian*, 9 October.

Painter, Nell Irvin. 1992. Hill, Thomas, and the use of racial stereotype. In *Race-ing Justice, En-Gendering Power: Essays on Anita Hill, Clarence Thomas, and the Construction of Social Reality*. Ed. Toni Morrison, 200–214. New York: Pantheon.

Perren, Alisa. 2012. *Indie, Inc: Miramax and the Transformation of Hollywood in the 1990s*. Austin: University of Texas Press.

Renov, Michael and Vincent Brook. 2017. Editorial introduction. In *From Shtetl to Stardom: Jews and Hollywood. (An Annual Review of the Casden Institute for the Study of the Jewish Role in American Life: Volume 14.)* Eds. Michael Renov and Vincent Brook, ix-xvi. West Lafayette: Purdue University Press.

Romero-Sánchez, Mónica, Barbara Krahé, Miguel Moya and Jesús L. Megías. 2018. Alcohol-related victim behaviour and rape myth acceptance as predictors of victim blame in sexual assault cases. *Violence Against Women* 24 (9): 1052–1069.

Romito, Patrizia. 2008. *A Deafening Silence – Hidden Violence Against Women and Children*. Bristol: Policy.

Ross, Andrew. 1992. The private parts of justice. In *Race-ing Justice, En-Gendering Power: Essays on Anita Hill, Clarence Thomas, and the Construction of Social Reality*. Ed. Toni Morrison, 40–60. New York: Pantheon

Ryan, Lisa. 2018. Christine Blasey Ford is still being put through hell. *The Cut*. 8 November. https://www.thecut.com/2018/11/kavanaugh-accuserchristine-blasey-ford-harassment.html. Accessed 27 November 2018.

Salter, Michael and Selda Dagistanli. 2015. Cultures of abuse: "sex grooming", organised abuse and race in Rochdale, UK. *International Journal for Crime, Justice and Social Democracy* 4(2): 50–64.

Sela-Shayovitz, Revital. 2015. "They are all good boys": the role of the Israeli media in the social construction of gang rape. *Feminist Media Studies* 15 (3): 411–428.

Shier, Allie and Eran Shor. 2016. "Shades of foreign evil": "honor killings" and "family murders": in the Canadian press. *Violence Against Women* 22 (10): 1163–1188.

Takla, Nefertiti. 2018. Reitman vs. Ronell: rethinking the role of gender and patri-archy in sexual harassment cases. *Bully Bloggers* (Blog). 7 September. https://bullybloggers.wordpress.com/2018/09/07/reitman-vs-ronell-rethinking-the-role-of-gender-and-patriarchy-in-sexual-harassment-cases/. Accessed 3 June 2019.

Walby, Sylvia, Jude Towers, Susie Balderston, Consuelo Corradi, Brian Francis, Markku Heiskanen, Karin Helweg-Larsen, Lut Mergaert, Philippa Olive, Emma Palmer, Heidi Stöckl and Sofia Strid. 2017. *The Concept and Measurement of Violence Against Women and Men*. Bristol: Policy Press.

Waterhouse-Watson, Deb. 2012. Framing the victim: sexual assault and Australian footballers on television. *Australian Feminist Studies* 27 (71): 55–70.

Waterhouse-Watson, Deb. 2013. *Athletes, Sexual Assault, and "Trials by Media"*. New York and London: Routledge.

Weinstein, Harvey. 2017. Statement. *New York Times*, 5 October.

Weiss, Karen G. 2010. Male sexual victimization: examining men's experiences of rape and sexual assault. *Men and Masculinities* 12 (3): 275–298.

Zacharek, Stephanie, Eliana Dockterman and Haley Sweetland Edwards. 2017. The silence breakers. *Time*, December.

Index[1]

[1] Note: Page numbers followed by 'n' refer to notes.

© The Author(s) 2019

K. Boyle, *#MeToo, Weinstein and Feminism*,

https://doi.org/10.1007/978-3-030-28243-1

CPI Antony Rowe
Eastbourne, UK
February 14, 2020